TAROT FOR FICTION WRITERS

Using the Cards to Supercharge Story Ideas, Deepen Characters, & Illuminate Plotlines

JESSICA ARDEN CLINE

WAYFARER

CONTENTS

To my Capitol Crimes writing community. Thanks for inspiring me and giving me a place to belong.

Welcome to Tarot for Fiction Writers

*Are you a **fiction writer** looking for a **fresh source of creativity**?

*Do you long to **recapture the joy and magic of storytelling**, but find yourself **hindered by perfectionism, stress, or a hectic life**?

*Do you need **a tool** to **help you start writing again after a hiatus or difficult time**?

*Are you a **neurodivergent writer** struggling to **start or finish creative projects** with your **executive function challenges**?

If you answered yes to any of those questions, I wrote this book for you.

Let ***Tarot for Fiction Writers*** help you rediscover the magic that first called you to write.

- Finish stalled projects.

- Get the dopamine power-up you need to initiate tasks and sustain motivation.

- Revolutionize your workflow with tarot-infused creativity.

HOW CAN THIS BOOK HELP ME?

Random and novel stimuli can amplify the creative process. You've probably had experiences where serendipity led to an idea that fired you up to get back to the keyboard. Maybe you went somewhere new and encountered a wine-drinking fountain next to one dispensing water[1] which led to an idea for a funny set piece in your fictional version of the afterlife.

Perhaps you spotted a church marquee whose letters had been scrambled to spell out a more irreverent and mischievous message. Suddenly, you've got the perfect story for a conversation between your two protagonists when one tells about his teenage prankster antics. Maybe you wandered into the room while your husband is watching a YouTube video of a couple building a secret passage with a genius opening mechanism, and bam! You know how the culprit got out of the locked room in your murder mystery.

Maybe you see a goth dude in his 50s rocking out on the subway, and when you exit the car, you hear classic NSYNC belting from his headphones. The experience reminds you of your 10th-grade crush who dressed much the same and inspired your Gregorian chant music phase.

You get the idea. Serendipitous moments charge up our creativity and lead us down fun and unexpected paths.

What if you could have the same experience with a deck of cards?

Focused brainstorming with tarot provides a resource of 78 cards, each with rich imagery and symbols that can also trigger distant associations and unconventional combinations of ideas when fused with your own.

When you use tarot, you don't have to wait for your next vacation or bide your time until one of these chance experiences sends the dominoes of your imagination cascading to solve a plot hole or character problem. You can simply bust out your deck anytime, shuffle, and create your own planned serendipity.

Tarot prompting isn't meant to replace moments of being in the world and discovering new things that inform your story. Many of the experiences we seek out and the people we encounter enrich our lives. Rather, think of tarot as a complement to these real-world experiences and a powerful, portable, always-available creative amplifier.

A Taste of What to Expect

Later in this book, we'll delve into more detail about how to make tarot prompting techniques work for you. But here's an activity to give you a taste of how tarot cards can spark your imagination.

For this exercise, let's work with the following elements to start us off:

Premise: A woman arrives home and finds her door ajar.

Genre: Choose your favorite genre.

Why is the always-locked door open? We're not sure and could use some help brainstorming ideas.

Imagine you pull out your tarot deck and draw the Temperance Card.

First, let's do a visual interpretation for ideas. Keeping your chosen genre and the premise above in mind, take a few minutes to look at the images and symbols on the Temperance card. What details do you notice? What kind of feeling do you get from the illustrations? What does each detail or the card as a whole make you think of? How can that relate to the story question: Why is the door ajar when the protagonist arrives home?

Got some ideas? Good.

Here are just a few examples of details you might pull from this card, followed by potential interpretations for each.

Imagery On the Temperance Card

- An angelic figure pouring liquid from one cup to another

- A glowing third eye in the center of her forehead

- Red wings

- A golden triangle patch on the angel's dress

- Still water

- Daffodils and other greenery growing all around the figure of the angel.

Example Interpretations for These Details

- An angelic figure pouring liquid from one golden cup to another.

  - A group of robbers disguised as missionaries have broken into her house.

  - She enters, and someone she's never seen before is mixing cocktails in her kitchen.

  - Her uber-religious estranged sibling has arrived unannounced and let themselves in.

  - Whatever she finds in the house settles it: it's time to undertake the quest for the holy grail.

- ○ A literal angel or other supernatural being (depending on your genre) has paid the protagonist a visit.

- A glowing third eye in the center of her forehead

  - ○ Your protagonist has a sudden premonition about the intruder.

  - ○ Someone with insight into her current problems has shown up unexpectedly.

- Red wings

  - ○ A sports fanatic really into the Detroit Red Wings has arrived.

  - ○ Seeing red and wings together makes you think of the slogan, "Red Bull gives you wings," which reminds you of the Red Bull mobile that used to park on your college campus to give out free samples. Maybe someone wild from the protagonist's college days shows up and upends her plans.

  - ○ The protagonist sees a trail of red feathers leading inside, deepening the mystery.

- A golden triangle patch on the angel's dress

  - ○ If this reminds you of a caution sign, your protagonist should proceed with caution.

  - ○ This symbol unearths a long-buried memory of your high school physics class and the memory that delta, a symbol shaped like a triangle, means change. Maybe a big change has arrived for your protagonist.

- Still water

  - ○ Your protagonist finds a trail of watery footprints leading to her kitchen.

- There's a flood, and a neighbor used their spare key to come in and try to stop it.

- Someone with a calming presence has arrived.

- Daffodils and other greenery growing all around the figure of the angel

  - Someone who once gave her flowers but now scares her has arrived.

  - She finds her gardener inside, saying he had to use the restroom. She's momentarily relieved, but why did he just come out of her bedroom?

  - A strange atmospheric mutation has caused an explosion of vines and plants to take over her house.

Keep in mind that there are no "right" answers. The best card-inspired brain-children are those that connect and resonate with your existing story ideas, yet lead you down fresh, unexpected paths.

Ideas from Traditional Card Meanings

You can also look at the card's traditional meaning for further insights and ideas.

The Temperance card in tarot typically represents balance, moderation, and harmony. Some of the key meanings associated with this card include:

- Balancing opposites or contrasting elements in one's life, such as the spiritual and the material, the masculine and the feminine, logic and emotions.

- Moderation, patience, and finding the middle ground rather than extremes.

- Healing, restoration, and the blending of different energies or aspects of the self.

- Adaptability, flexibility, and the ability to go with the flow.

- Finding the right mix or proportion between different forces or aspects of life.

Spend a few minutes reading and considering this card's meaning in the context of our story question and your chosen genre. What phrases or ideas jump out at you? Who or what do they make you think of? How could elements of this meaning apply to the story? How do these ideas build on or lead you down a different path than your visual interpretations?

Some Examples of Ideas You Could Pull from this Traditional Meaning:

- The person who's arrived will make the protagonist realize how much she's let her life get out of balance and set off her character arc.

- An injured person has hidden inside the protagonist's house and needs healing.

- The person who's arrived will help the regimented, orderly protagonist learn to adapt and live in the moment.

- A person the protagonist had a contentious relationship with in the past shows up, and despite butting heads, through the course of the story, they learn to balance their extremes and fall in love.

- A villain bent on restoring order and balance to the world by their twisted logic is hunting your protagonist and has broken into her house.

After this example, you should have a sense of how tarot prompting can help you brainstorm creative ideas for your stories. How did you feel going through that exercise? If it piqued your interest or inspired you to learn more, please read on.

1. . This actually exists at a winery in Northern Spain. My husband and I discovered it and availed ourselves of both fountains while walking the Camino de Santiago years ago.

INTRODUCTION: WHEN THE MUSE HAS LEFT THE CHAT

CREATIVITY has entered the chat.

Shiny new idea! Let's do this.

Ooh, and what about this?

Let's add this!

Brilliant!

Creative bliss activated.

Entering flow state.

…

…

Uh oh. We're slowing down.

SELF DOUBT has entered the chat.

EXECUTIVE FUNCTION CHALLENGES have entered the chat.

The newness is wearing off. HELP.

DISTRACTIONS have entered the chat.

STRESS has entered the chat.

UNEXPECTED LIFE EVENT has entered the chat.

Running low on energy. But must keep going,

How am I supposed to write when I feel like this???

DEADLINES have entered the chat.

OK, we can rally. Can't let everyone down.

Must make every word count.

Work smarter, not harder, right?

PERFECTIONISM has entered the chat.

CRIPPLING SELF-DOUBT has entered the chat.

NOSTALGIA has entered the chat.

Remember the early days of this project when we were excited and inspired?

We couldn't wait to get back to the page.

If you're reading this book, you've probably been there. After all, being a writer often means vacillating between delusions of grandeur and crippling self-doubt.

The highs are heady. You *made* something Out of nothing. A whole book! Or a short story. An idea. A scene that perfectly captured the one from your mind. Characters that bring their imperfect, dinged-up selves to the page and muster the courage to catch the killer, save the world, approach the person of their dreams, or confront their abuser.

These are the parts we live for. The bits that sustain us and keep us coming back to the page. Even when we feel discouraged or get a critical review.

Because creative work can be intensely personal, it feels like part of our identity. Not so much a job as a vocation. Part of our "muchness." There's a reason Hemingway likens writing to opening a vein and bleeding on the page.

It follows that for storytellers, the ability to tap into creativity is essential—not just for our writing projects but also for our sense of self and purpose.

When the stress of deadlines, isolation, burnout, and life challenges conspire to sap our emotional reserves and the motivation necessary to create, no wonder it shakes us.

Even for those of us who view creativity as a vital part of ourselves, there will be times when the ideas dry up. The Muse gets crowded out by the realities of the day job, care-taking responsibilities, grief, burnout, anxiety, sickness, chronic pain, brain fog, etc.

It's not fair. It's not ideal. Especially when we're on deadline. Unfortunately, the hard truth is there will be times for almost all of us when the writing grinds to a halt, gets put on the back burner, or only happens in fits and starts, relegated to the scraps of time we can pull together.

When this happens, as many of you well know, it can be incredibly destabilizing.

And even worse, the longer it continues, the more fear and self-doubt can stage a pile-on that would put any social media mob to shame.

In this head space, we fret we'll never write anything good again and no one will remember us. Won't we lose all our momentum on a new series if we don't get a new book out ASAP? And as much as we remind ourselves that comparison is the thief of joy, it's hard not to notice that so and so has written and published two or four or ten books while we've been stalled.

The most unfortunate thing about this thought spiral is that it puts us into a scarcity mindset. When limping along with scant energy and attention, we're often desperate to catch up, meet deadlines, and trounce our FOMO. Time feels fleeting, and our desire to live up to our expectations can create a mindset that insists we make every moment count. We strive to get each word perfect the first time. No room for mistakes or experiments.

Ironically, this makes our brains lock up and inhibits the kind of divergent thinking that produces novel and exciting combinations. Why? Besides the negative toll on our mental and physical health, this state of mind is exactly the opposite of what we need to produce our best creative work. According to the American Psychological Association, stress can also interfere with our ability to think clearly and creatively. While a certain amount of stress can be beneficial and even spur us into action, higher stress-levels trigger the brain to shift both physiological and cognitive resources to more urgent needs: hypervigilance and survival.

This laser-focus on survival forces other parts of the brain, including those involved in creative decision-making, to rely on well-known categories and patterns to conserve energy. In these conditions, our brains rule out anything risky or off-the-wall. We stick to the sure things. The tried and true. The middle of the road. The low-hanging fruit.

When stress becomes chronic, these conditions can continue over time, blocking access to unconventional thinking in the name of survival. We're more likely to stick with the same old approach even when it's not working. In addition to personal stressors, I doubt many of us came out of the past few years of a global pandemic, the corresponding lockdowns, mounting racial violence, and a climate of political extremes unscathed. It's okay if you struggled then. It's okay if you wrote like crazy to cope with the state of the world and had a delayed crash and burnout. It's okay if you're *still* struggling.

But how do we dig ourselves out of this miserable, unsustainable place and get back to the joy of writing?

The good news is that there are strategies to help redirect our brains towards a state that's more conducive to creativity. These strategies allow our minds to open to innovative ideas and maximize more flexible ways of thinking. The practice of tarot prompting incorporates three strategies: play, randomness, and novelty. It also capitalizes on the archetypes and story cycles embedded in tarot.

My Story

In the last half of 2022, I was feeling a lot like this guy.

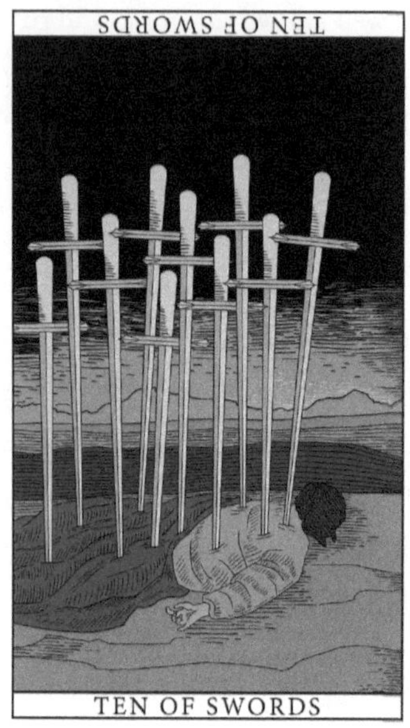

You know those stress index tests that ask about the major adverse or disruptive events you've experienced lately and give you a score? If stress and upheaval were an Olympic sport, I would've been on the podium.

In the previous two years, my life had been thrown into even more chaos than usual. In July 2020, I left Las Vegas, my beloved hometown of twenty-plus years. With this transition, I also gave up a rare full-time teaching position in my field, along with all my family, friends, and community there.

I'd planned to make the most of the months leading up to the move, spending time with loved ones while they were still just a short drive away.

Of course, in March 2020, that plan went out the window with the arrival of Covid-19 and the associated lockdowns.

In case you were wondering, moving in the middle of a global pandemic sucks. Despite being an introvert, I'm a very social person, and connection with others feeds my soul. I'd hoped to meet new people through writing organizations once I'd moved and had scouted out Sacramento-area groups. Plus, I held onto the prospect of seeing friends soon since both the Romance Writers of America National Convention and Bouchercon (a crime and mystery writers convention) were scheduled in San Francisco and Sacramento for the fall of that year.

The transition hit hard. Despite being incredibly fortunate to have moved with and near family, I still grieved the loss of face-to-face connections with my Las Vegas people and the avenues to make new friends that were snatched away by circumstances out of my control.

My depression and anxiety worsened from both the personal and collective trauma of the time. My husband got put on a project that required him to live three hours away for most of the week, leaving me alone with my two boys in an unfamiliar city. Other turbulent parenting and family challenges and events followed in this time span. But I kept pushing through. What else could I do?

By some miracle, I managed to write and publish a book by the fall of 2021. That book was my creative outlet and my solace. I poured all my grief over missing my friends, losing my beloved grandma without getting to say goodbye, and everything else into it.

But after that, while trying to write the sequel, I hit a hard stop. My writing slowed to drips and drabs no matter how much I sat my butt in the chair. My mind wandered. Brain fog crept in even more than usual. I lost the joy of it all, engulfed by anger, disconnection, and a sense of abandonment by my writing mojo.

In hindsight, of course, this moment was coming. It was the perfect tempest of prolonged turbulence, tension, and uncertainty. I'd pushed through on empty for too long, and at last, I'd tapped out. I was in survival mode, and my brain had gone on strike.

But I wasn't going down without a fight. The loss of my creative outlet along with everything else, was a step too far. I tried short stories, shifting focus to other artistic endeavors like graphic design, desperately trying to claw my way to a place where I could write again. When pandemic restrictions eased, I joined Capitol Crimes, my local chapter of Sisters in Crime, volunteered, and started to meet some friends.

Soon after, in the process of getting my youngest son diagnosed with ADHD, I learned that the condition presented differently in girls and women and realized how many of the classic markers I had as well. This led to my own diagnosis and treatment. The new framework of understanding my brain was revelatory for me and explained so much about my emotional dysregulation, impulsivity, and the way my mind either jumped around from one thing to another like a pinball on speed or got stuck in hyperfocus mode.

I was sure these things would be the key to getting me writing again. And they did. More, at least, but I was still putting a lot of pressure on myself to tell a good story and get it right the first time.

Then, in the fall of 2022, Lisa Kessler spoke to my local chapter of Sisters in Crime and mentioned using tarot cards as prompts for writing. That struck me as a brilliant idea. Story structure is baked into the progression of the cards. There's so much symbolism, and messy emotions in the card meanings that could stir up ideas to give characters more depth. Plus, so many archetypes are present in the tarot.

I immediately signed up for Lisa's class on the subject (which I highly recommend), but it didn't start for another two months. So, in the intervening weeks, I was so inspired and galvanized by the idea and the possibilities that I amassed a collection of tarot decks and began devising ways to use them in my writing.

After being stalled for so long, the process re-energized me, pushed my stories in exciting directions, and planted whole nurseries full of seeds for new ones. That joy of creating that I'd been missing bubbled up to the surface again.

At some point during the last year, I realized I'd filled multiple notebooks with spread notes, prompt ideas, and insights on this practice, along with the brain science behind it.

I knew that this had the potential to help other fiction writers as much as it helped me. Because as much desire and willpower as we pour into creating, the reality is there will still be forces pushing against us. When this happens, it may take time to come back to writing, but when you do, I want you to have as many tools as possible to push back and reconnect with your creative side. I decided to create a resource others could turn to when feeling stuck, stalled, burned out, or trapped in the clutches of perfectionism.

You may find yourself in these situations, in need of a resource to spice things up and get you laying the foundations of story again. But whether you're starting from a place of burnout or just want a playful strategy to help add depth to your stories and get you unstuck, the tarot techniques in this book can serve as a beneficial tool to get you writing and stretching your imagination.

Part One

Before We Get Started

CHAPTER 1.1
BEFORE WE GET STARTED

WHO THIS BOOK IS FOR

This book is designed for tarot-curious fiction writers. Specifically, it aims to help writers in these three categories:

- Writers searching for something fun to spark creativity.

- Writers coming back to the page after a hiatus. Perhaps you've lost the magic because of burnout, stress, unexpected life events, perfectionism, or self-doubt.

- Neurodivergent writers who need a novel approach to start or renew focus on longer projects.

Tarot prompting can be beneficial for plotters, discovery writers, and anyone in between. The book contains prompts on characters, big-picture plotting, and prompts to get you unstuck at any point in your WIP.

WHAT IF I'M NOT A "WOO-WOO" PERSON? ARE WE USING THE CARDS FOR FORTUNE-TELLING?

Nope! Although tarot spreads can be used for divination, we're using the cards for an entirely different purpose. The only fates and juicy revelations we'll uncover are those concerning your characters.

The techniques outlined here involve drawing from and combining symbolism, visual cues, and other aspects of the card to spur new ideas, deepen and enrich your stories, and send your brain on unexpected paths. As you'll learn in a later section, there's even neurological research showing that using random visual cues like the ones in the cards can help you access a far broader range of memories and associations than working in isolation.

If you're comfortable using visual or text prompts or even asking a friend for something random to add to a story, you'll likely find the process familiar. The bonus of working with a deck of 78 cards is that it's more robust than many other types of visual prompting.

Both skeptics and those drawn to the mystical can benefit from the exercises in this book.

DO I HAVE TO MEMORIZE ALL THE CARD MEANINGS?

No. Though you may go down a tarot rabbit hole after working with these techniques like I did, it's unnecessary to memorize card meanings. Even when I know a card's meaning, I almost always still look up interpretations in several tarot guidebooks to gain extra nuggets of insight and perspective.

The Storytellers' Tarot Reference Guide at the end of this book contains all 78 card meanings, as well as how each card might be interpreted in terms of character traits, plot, theme, and character and relationship conflicts. It also includes sections on numerology and common symbolism in tarot.

Most tarot decks include guidebooks as well. I love to read each author's unique spin on the cards' traditional meanings. You can also use free online tarot guides like the one at Tarot.com.

DO I HAVE TO BUY A TAROT DECK TO USE THE EXERCISES IN THIS BOOK?

I highly recommend working with a deck of your own to get the most out of tarot prompting. Working with a physical deck will allow you to view multiple cards in a spread simultaneously, which will help you spot similarities and connections between them. The tactile experience of working with the cards and a notebook can also be grounding and keep the temptation of online notifications and distractions at bay.

However, if you want to give it a go before buying a deck, check out an online tarot randomizer site like https://randomtarotcard.com/.

WHY ME? YOUR TAROT GUIDE, JESSICA ARDEN CLINE

As I shared in the introduction, incorporating tarot cards into my writing process over the past year and a half has been a game-changer. It took me from a place of disconnection and burnout and threw me a lifeline to make writing playful and joyful again. With this resource, I hope to pass that lifeline along to you.

Though I've only been using tarot for brainstorming connected to writing for the past few years, my experience with the cards, as well as creative writing and teaching, goes back much further.

I picked up my first deck of tarot cards over twenty years ago while studying abroad in San Sebastian, Spain. I'd been assigned a how-to speech for my communications class. While musing on potential topics, I wandered into a charming shop amidst the bars with Basque names and restaurants in Parte Vieja, where a deck of tarot cards captured my attention.

The cards have always fascinated me. I loved it when they would turn up in movies and books and send a story spinning in a new direction. I was drawn to their stories and hidden meanings, so I decided that was the perfect time to learn more and teach my classmates too with my speech.

Since then, my interest in tarot has endured. I've sprinkled tarot elements into nearly all my fiction. Readings and cards have appeared everywhere, from meet-cutes to portents of how a paranormal cozy mystery would play out.

In addition to my interest in the cards and my love of creative writing, teaching has always been a passion of mine. I did my MEd in Curriculum and Instruction and have spent over fifteen years as an educator in university, community, and corporate settings, working with individuals and even creating training modules for PBS. I've also given many workshops and presentations in the realm of academia and writing, including workshops focused on Tarot for Fiction Writers.

With my teaching and curriculum design background, I've set out to create a useful, engaging, and accessible guide to help anyone with a background in storytelling get started with tarot.

CHAPTER 1.2
WHAT TO EXPECT FROM THIS BOOK

This book contains everything you'll need to get started with incorporating tarot prompting into your writing practice, except your deck. Here's a breakdown of what's in store in this shiny new tool to help you reconnect with your creative spark. Feel free to jump around to the parts that interest you most.

SECTION 1: INTRO TO CREATIVE TAROT PROMPTING

Part 1: Intro and Before We Get Started

Part 2: The Tarot for Fiction Writers Approach

Part 3: Intro to the Tarot and How Tarot Can Supercharge Your Creative Process

In the first three parts, you'll learn what tarot prompting is and how it works with your imagination and subconscious to spark new connections. This section also contains background on the major parts of tarot decks and the cards' connections to universal human experiences, archetypes, and story cycles.

SECTION 2: TAROT PROMPTING IN ACTION

Part 4: Getting Started with Tarot Prompts: Step-by-Step Instructions

Part 5: Tarot Prompt Library

Part 6: Interpreting the Cards

This section walks you through the entire process from identifying the story help you need, choosing a prompt, using the cards, and interpreting cards for story ideas.

Part 4 provides step-by-step instructions on how to use the cards to add depth to your narratives and help you get unstuck.

The prompt library in Part 5 contains over 200 prompts tailored to different aspects of storytelling: Character and Relationship Prompts, Plot, Setting, and Worldbuilding Prompts, and Prompts to Get you Unstuck.

Part 6 offers guidance on different ways to interpret the cards along with example interpretations.

SECTION 3: THE STORYTELLERS TAROT REFERENCE GUIDE

Part 7: The Storytellers Tarot Reference Guide
Part 8: Conclusion

Finally, Part 7 contains The Storytellers Tarot Reference Guide. Here you'll find the traditional meanings of each of the 78 tarot cards, with added dimensions for storytelling. Each entry contains ideas for how the card could be interpreted in terms of character traits, themes, plot, story conflict, and relationship conflict. Part 7 also contains sections on tarot numerology and common symbols found in the tarot and their meanings.

Part eight will leave you with some final thoughts.

Let's get started.

Part Two

THE TAROT FOR FICTION WRITERS APPROACH

YOUR IMAGINATION +
HIGH-IMPACT STORYTELLING PROMPTS +
TAROT INTERPRETATION

THE TAROT FOR FICTION WRITERS APPROACH

TAROT PROMPTING, RANDOMNESS, AND EVADING THE EFFICIENCY PRINCIPLE

Imagine you're working on a psychological thriller and have the basic idea for the story, but some specifics keep eluding you. You know your protagonist Katherine's neighbor Gretchen insinuates herself into Katherine's life. You want her to do so through a series of acts that could be taken as kind and neighborly but become increasingly menacing. You sit at your desk and brainstorm what those could be, but everything you come up with feels uninspired or suspiciously similar to events from the last few novels you've read or your most recent binge-watch.

Finally, after an hour of getting nowhere, you take a gym break to clear your head. As you get moving on the elliptical, music plays, and you open your book about a neuroscientist's studies on canine decision-making. Various TV screens overhead broadcast programs you might not choose at home: a cooking competition show, something on HGTV, the news, an infomercial for Emeril Lagasse's new line of unbreakable stainless-steel pans, and the movie *Freaky Friday*.

You pedal on with your story question still fresh in your mind and let your attention wander between your book and the assorted programs. While exposed to these different inputs that aren't usually found together, new ideas start to cross-pollinate and bubble up. You read a fascinating tidbit on dog psychology, and a golden retriever pup and a sheepdog bound onto the renovation show to greet the carpenter. The host jokes the dogs love the carpenter more than they love her. Your imagination sparks at this—instead of working in real estate, what if the scheming neighbor was some kind of dog whisperer or animal psychic? She could put her plan in motion by winning over Katherine's unruly puppy first. That's definitely a more interesting angle. Who could distrust a dog lover?

With that thought brewing, your attention pans to a beautiful field of buttercups on the news. You'd already decided that Katherine was an avid gardener and especially took pride in her flowers. What if her puppy destroyed them—either at the neighbor's coaxing or because it was playing and didn't know better? That could give the neighbor an immediate in with Katherine's family by offering to help train the puppy. As your workout continues, you gather even more possibilities from the scenes in front of you. Someone drills Emeril's pan to demonstrate its indestructibility—a possible murder weapon? Or maybe Katherine is a horrible cook and isn't much help to her teen daughter who dreams of culinary school. The neighbor could invite the daughter for cooking lessons and drive a wedge between the mother and daughter.

The sight of the Lindsay Lohan and Jamie Lee Curtis body-swap plot spins your thoughts in yet another direction. The neighbor's plotting to get Katherine out of the way and take up with her husband and daughter. But what if Katherine secretly feels stifled in her life and would gladly trade places? The two women could cook up a plan for them to both get what they want.

You've probably experienced a similar phenomenon while traveling to an unfamiliar destination, overhearing strangers' conversations in a coffee shop, or exploring someplace new, even within your familiar territory. Exposure to a new environment or new stimuli shifts your perspective. In *The Artist's Way*, Julia Cameron prescribes a weekly artist's date, in which you take yourself out somewhere new for a few hours and take time to observe and reflect. The reason this practice is so effective for creative renewal is that by giving your mind random outside resources to bounce ideas against, you're able to reach far beyond the more common associations that come up while working in isolation.

Tarot prompting works in a similar way, leveraging unfamiliar and unexpected stimuli from your environment. You start with your imagination and reflect on a story question, whether that's something like, *What's the secret from this character's past they don't want anyone to know?* Or *What's something unexpected that could happen in the next scene?* Keeping this question in mind, you shuffle your deck and draw cards to spark ideas for possible solutions. As you consider your chosen cards, the imagery, symbols, or traditional meanings can trigger associations from past experiences, pull from your subconscious, and help you make unexpected and delightful connections with your existing story ideas.

Sounds intuitive enough. But there's also a scientific basis for how this type of process can make us more creative. Taking a process like creative ideation that is usually done in isolation and adding an interactive component actually changes the way our brain comes up with ideas and has two especially powerful effects.

The first is an **expanded capacity for creativity and novelty**. Adding an unfamiliar component to the creative process activates what scientists refer to as a semantic search of one's memories. This signals your brain to pull from a broader range of associations stored in your memory, including those that are distant, long forgotten, or tucked away in your subconscious.

Introducing an outside element into the brainstorming process can also help writers overcome what's known as the brain's **efficiency principle**. This is excellent news for those struggling to get past cliché and the most obvious solutions to story problems.

The human brain has a dizzying number of responsibilities and a finite amount of energy to work with. It's no surprise that over time, the brain develops shortcuts to streamline processing to save energy wherever possible. This is fabulous for our ability to make sense of the constant barrage of sensory input or to quickly determine if the animal bounding toward our campsite is a baby bear or an incredibly large dog.

However, this efficiency principle cultivates an automaticity in thought patterns that works against creative thinking. The powerful biological drive to save energy means that it takes shortcuts when possible. Because relying on and reinforcing well-known patterns conserves energy, there's a powerful biological drive to rely on those well-tread pathways.

Throwing something new into the mix can help our imaginations wander beyond the obvious and subvert the efficiency principle. Random chance serves as a catalyst that can break us free from fixed patterns of thinking and broaden our available range of imaginative possibilities.

Another delightful benefit of adding an outside element to interact with while creating is that this can lead to faster solutions. Yes, you read that right. As David Kirsh, Professor and past Chair of the Department of Cognitive Science at the University of California at San Diego, concludes in his article "The Importance of Chance and Interactivity in Creativity:" "**Interactive thinkers reach solutions faster** than individuals thinking on their own"(Norman 1993; Kirsh and Maglio 1994).

This is possible because some processes that would typically require internal handling, such as devising every detail of a plot, characters' back stories, and relationship dynamics, get performed externally. Associations prompted by a visual cue like a symbol or image on a tarot card are easier to access more rapidly.

THE POWER OF PLAY FOR YOUR WRITING PRACTICE

"I don't think it's too much to say that play can save your life."
- Dr. Stuart Brown from *Play: How it Shapes the Brain, Opens the Imagination, and Invigorates the Soul*

Another brilliant thing about using the Tarot for Fiction Writers approach is that it helps our brains slip into a state of play. Play can be crucial for creative renewal, stress relief, and overall well-being. It can also provide a low-stakes way to return to writing after a hiatus or period of burnout.

Even if we know the benefits, it can be difficult to access this playful state in trying times. Besides dealing with pressure—both from ourselves and others—we live in a culture that values productivity and output. There's an unconscious expectation that we must be serious about our work, pushing past sickness and personal issues to keep going at all costs. There's even a note of morality attached. Working through hardships: good. Rest and play: weak and frivolous.

In the Western world, the attitudes born from the industrial revolution and the protestant work ethic linger in our psyches, creating this additional pressure. They persist in the form of hustle culture that glorifies mad genius CEOs who work 80+ hours a week and sleep in their offices.

This legacy carries toxic consequences. It also creates mental stumbling blocks for creatives whose work dances across the lines between work, play, and vocation. Even when we intuitively know that play supports creativity, we still have to push back against the protestant work ethic devil on our shoulder who whispers that proper writing looks like toiling away at the keyboard faithfully at 5 AM each day and producing something of substance.

If that method works for you, great. But don't forget that writing can also look like sitting in a park at the edge of the woods daydreaming. It can look like going to a museum or the theater or wandering through the city, stopping for a coffee, and jotting down ideas. It can look like intense bouts of focus followed by down time that gives your brain the mental white space to connect and process ideas. It can look like storyboarding. Or acting out your ideas with Barbies (there's a great Writing Excuses podcast episode about a co-writing duo that does this). Or talking through your plot with a friend.

Writing can also look like playing with tarot cards. This exercise comes with an additional advantage that tips our minds into play. Using cards, objects traditionally used for gameplay, cues our brains that we're about to let loose and have fun.

After receiving that cue, the brain shifts into a physiological mode where the stakes are low. This playful mindset creates a safe space to explore and get messy. This is a wonderful zone for creative work because it allows us to experiment with new perspectives, unconventional scenarios, and narrative tasks without the pressure of performance anxiety.

The fluid, open-ended nature of play also encourages flexibility of thought. It emboldens our imagination to consider new possibilities. While playing, we're more likely to take creative risks and switch between thoughts, which increases the likelihood of making new connections and working beyond our status quo. Paradoxically, taking time to incorporate play into the writing process can make us *more* productive.

NOVELTY, DOPAMINE, CREATIVITY, AND MOTIVATION

A third way that working with tarot prompts can re-energize writers is through novelty. Introducing something **shiny and new** to the writing process can help battle stagnation and also serves as a powerful strategy to activate neurodivergent minds.

New experiences, sights, processes, objects, or people can make our brains happy. When we ride a roller coaster, learn how to make sourdough, dye our hair purple, or try a friend's flavorful homemade curry for the first time, our brains release a neurotransmitter called dopamine.

Dopamine, sometimes called the feel-good neurotransmitter, stimulates the parts of the brain in charge of emotions, behaviors, goal-setting, and motivation.

This is why novelty is an important tool to employ when you're feeling bored with a story or spinning your wheels on the same old ideas. Seeking out new experiences can give you that mood-boosting dopamine to get you moving again. Dopamine also fuels goal-directed behavior like finishing a novel and jump-starts motivation.

While novelty is an impactful tool for all creatives, it's especially beneficial for those of us with ADHD and others with executive function challenges.

Executive functions are like the control center operators of the brain. They're in charge of the skills that help us plan, oversee, and complete tasks.

Some executive functioning skills include:

- regulating attention and focus,

- task initiation,

- planning, organizing, prioritizing, progress-monitoring, and completion of plans,

- working memory,

- emotional regulation, and

- flexible thinking

For many, the realization a writing task is important can be enough to get started. However, for us ADHDers, there's an additional roadblock involving the brain's dopamine system.

In an "average" or neurotypical brain, just the understanding that something needs to be done triggers the release of dopamine, which motivates action. The dopamine is then reabsorbed once the task is completed.

However, people with ADHD have differences in their dopamine re-uptake systems that can create roadblocks to sustaining motivation and attention.

Even when ADHDers know a writing task is important, our brains may release less attention-sustaining dopamine. Or the dopamine that is released gets burned through and reabsorbed much more quickly.

This leads to two main issues that can affect writing and the ability to complete creative projects:

Low motivation: Without the surge of dopamine to propel them into action, ADHDers experience difficulties starting tasks that require sustained effort, like writing.

Inability to focus: The dopamine that is released doesn't remain at adequate levels for as long as needed. Especially when a task is long, tedious, or lacks variety. This makes it hard to maintain attention and focus on prolonged or mundane writing activities.

Introducing novelty can help us bridge those gaps in motivation and focus.

A steady diet of new activities and experiences can help create and sustain motivation over the long term. Gamification of tasks and play are also helpful strategies.

The new experiences needn't be extravagant, like a spa day or a trip to Tokyo. Something as simple as trying an unusual fruit from a new grocery store can do the trick. Watching a TV show outside your usual genre, trying to write a poem as a writing warm-up, or grabbing a deck of tarot cards can feed this desire for novelty too.

Tarot prompting provides a fun, fresh approach to brainstorming with 78 cards, each rich in imagery, symbolism, and meaning that can be used in endless combinations to spark new ideas for your stories. And because the novelty wears off faster for the neurodivergent among us, collecting new decks over time can help keep things fresh.

When you use the cards for story ideas, novelty, randomness, and play, work in concert to create the conditions where your creative spirit can venture out to play. It's a space with potential for positive emotions, where you can sidestep judgment (at least temporarily). It's a place where you can access distant associations and mine your subconscious for unexpected connections. A place that forces a shift in perspective that can increase creativity and nudge us out of our comfort zones.

A Shift in Perspective

PART THREE

INTRO TO THE TAROT

HOW TAROT
CAN SUPERCHARGE
YOUR CREATIVE PROCESS

CHAPTER 3.1
INTRO TO THE TAROT

Before we work with tarot prompts, here's a brief primer on the basics. The Tarot is a deck of playing cards that has been used for centuries for divination, meditation, and self-reflection. Its roots in storytelling date back to the Italian and European Renaissance.

Early tarot decks were made for game play. It wasn't until the 1700s that occultist Jean-Baptiste Alliette (aka Etteilla) developed and popularized the use of cards for divination. Then in 1909, British artist, writer, illustrator, and occultist Pamela Colman Smith[1] along with co-creator Arthur Waite, occultist, magazine editor, and Freemason, developed the deck that is still most widely used today: The Rider-Waite-Smith Deck [2].

Today, a quick internet search will turn up a plethora of decks with beautiful illustrations, some incorporating much of the traditional symbolism developed by Colman Smith and Waite and others following their own path of interpretation.

There are 78 cards in a tarot deck. These cards are divided into two main groups: the Major Arcana and the Minor Arcana. The Major Arcana contains 22 cards, numbered from 0 (The Fool) to 21 (the World), while the Minor Arcana has 56 cards. The Minor Arcana cards are further divided into four suits: Cups, Wands, Swords, and Pentacles. Fourteen cards appear in every suit (1-10 plus four court cards). Each card carries a unique symbolism and message, making this a robust tool to help generate associations and ideas to get your story flowing.

---

1. Some more fun facts about Pamela Coleman Smith: Known as "Pixie," Pamela was also biracial, born to a Jamaican mother and white American father. She joined a traveling theater troupe after attending art school at the Pratt Institute in NYC and garnered a reputation for her skill with costume and set design as well as her work on stage. Her illustrations were featured in the works of William Butler Yates and Bram Stoker and later in her own collection of Jamaican folktales. Pamela was also active in the women's suffrage movement.

2. Also traditionally called the Rider-Waite deck because why would you credit a female creative in the early 1900s? The Rider part of Rider-Waite Smith refers to the original publisher of the deck, William Rider and Sons of London.

WHY TAROT PROMPTING IS A STORYTELLER'S DREAM: STORY CYCLES AND ARCHETYPES

Most of us have memories of reading a book and coming across a passage that made us feel like the author was speaking directly to us and our experience. Those profound moments of feeling understood and less alone are often what inspire us to tell stories and pay that experience forward to others.

Nearly all of us aim to craft arresting stories and characters that create that kind of deep connection with readers. The tarot is a perfect prompting tool to round out your stories and help you get there. Why?

Because of the built-in story cycles, universal challenges, fears, longings, obstacles, experiences, and conflicting emotions that are captured in the cards. Not to mention the rich imagery, colors, symbols, and numbers found on the cards that can spark our imaginations. Drawing inspiration from the cards can help us pull in elements for more resonant plots, character arcs, and multi-dimensional characters.

We humans are a messy bunch and often compare our insides to other people's curated outsides. When we allow our characters and stories to reflect our strengths along with our flaws, contradictions, and insecurities, it can be a powerful way to forge connections with readers. The cards can remind us to explore additional facets of character that we might have overlooked on our own.

DIGGING INTO A CHARACTER'S PSYCHE: THE COLLECTIVE UNCONSCIOUS, ARCHETYPES, AND INDIVIDUATION

Swiss psychologist and psychiatrist Carl Gustav Jung's work didn't rise to prominence until after the publication of the Rider-Waite-Smith tarot deck. However, there is still a surprising amount of alignment between the concepts and symbols on the cards and Jung's principles in analytical psychology.

This can help us go deeper into the mental and emotional lives of our characters.

THE COLLECTIVE UNCONSCIOUS

One of Jung's theories concerns the idea of a collective unconscious, a part of the unconscious mind that all humans share. Imagine, somewhere in a hidden nook of your brain resides a grand *Beauty and the Beast*-scale library populated with memories, behavior patterns, primal instincts, and collective traumas passed down from generation to generation.

Jung believed that tucked away in these stacks were blueprints or archetypes that included universal themes and figures, such as the Hero, the Mother, and the Trickster. These show up across cultures in dreams, myths, and tales.

If you're familiar with Theodora Taylor's work on universal fantasies, those patterns also align with the idea of a collective unconscious.

In Jung's framework, the collective unconscious can have a significant influence on norms and behaviors and provides a template for psychological development.

The progression of cards in the Major Arcana, aka The Fool's Journey, lays out a cyclical map for psychological development.

STORY CYCLES, CHARACTER ARCS, AND THE FOOL'S JOURNEY

The process of what Jung terms **individuation** is like a **character arc**. It's a journey toward healing, wholeness, and self-realization. This happens through encounters with archetypal themes and images that challenge our beliefs and abilities. These challenges help integrate the hidden aspects of our characters and ourselves with the conscious aspects to become whole.

Even though the originators of the tarot lived far before Jung's day, this cycle plays out in the Fool's Journey through the cards in the Major Arcana.

If you're familiar with the Hero's Journey, popularized by Joseph Campbell and later Christopher Vogler, or the Heroine's Journey, eknumerated by Maureen Murdock, and recently written about by Gail Carriger, you'll spot quite a few parallels in the Fool's Journey through the Major Arcana in the Tarot.

EMBARKING ON THE JOURNEY

The Major Arcana is made up of the first twenty-two cards in the tarot, from (0) The Fool to (21) The World. In this card progression, The Fool, the avatar for your protagonist, sets off on a new adventure, meets allies and enemies, faces challenges and setbacks, and gains the hard-earned wisdom necessary for the culmination of their story. Sound familiar yet?

If your book has a happy ending, The World is where your main character(s) find purpose and meaning from the events they've weathered along the way.

Traditionally, **the Major Arcana** represents **big-picture life events**. I like to think of them as milestone cards. Each one represents a tent-pole moment or contact with a person set to have a significant impact on your character and story as it unfolds.

There are two primary ways to utilize the Major Arcana cards to generate story ideas. First, you can use the Fool's Journey and the Major Arcana as a whole to create a story framework. If you like to plan stories and know the major beats of your preferred structure, Major Arcana cards are great for helping expand on the important events and figures in your story.

Second, Major Arcana cards can be pulled individually as part of any chosen prompt. Those of you who discover the story as you go can use the Major Arcana to liven up your chapters or derail your characters along the way. If you know you need a big moment, separate the Major Arcana from the rest of the deck and pull from that stack.

Here's a breakdown of what the Fool's Journey looks like card-by-card. After the description of each card's beat or important figure, you'll find an example of that beat in action in *The Hunger Games* by Suzanne Collins.

One thing to note: the steps don't have to be followed strictly in this order, as you'll see in the example.

THE FOOL'S JOURNEY IN ACTION

0. THE FOOL - THE STORY BEGINS WITH THE FOOL, REPRESENTING INNOCENCE AND NEW BEGINNINGS. THE FOOL IS ABOUT TO EMBARK ON A JOURNEY. THIS IS LIKE THE BEGINNING OF A HERO'S JOURNEY STORY.

The Hunger Games opens with Katniss Everdeen, a young girl who supports her family living in poverty in District 12. She's about to have her life upended when she volunteers to take her sister's place as a tribute in the Hunger Games, an event where young people must fight to the death for the entertainment of the elite. This marks the beginning of her hero's journey.

1. THE MAGICIAN - THE FOOL ENCOUNTERS A WISE FIGURE, THE MAGICIAN, WHO HELPS THEM PREPARE FOR THE JOURNEY AHEAD. THE MAGICIAN REPRESENTS KNOWLEDGE, POWER, AND GUIDANCE.

Haymitch Abernathy, a past District 12 victor, helps Katniss prepare for the games by giving advice and guidance. He participated in the games before and came home with the specialized knowledge about what it takes to survive the vicious game.

2. THE HIGH PRIESTESS - THE FOOL ENCOUNTERS THE HIGH PRIESTESS, A MYSTERIOUS AND INTUITIVE FIGURE REPRESENTING SECRETS AND THE SUBCONSCIOUS. THIS IS LIKE ENCOUNTERING A MENTOR FIGURE.

Katniss's stylist, Cinna, lets her in on the secrets to charming the Capitol elite as a means to garner favor. Though she wants none of the pomp and circumstance of smiling for the cameras, Cinna shows her how creating a persona can aid in her determination to win the game and get back to her sister.

3. The Empress - The Empress represents motherhood, fertility, and nurturing. The Fool experiences birth and new life.

Cinna also serves as a nurturing figure who helps create her new persona as the "girl on fire." Katniss is reborn as a tribute who must now fight for her life in front of all of Panem.

4. The Emperor - The Emperor represents authority, structure, and stability. The Fool encounters rules and order.

Katniss enters the arena and must follow the rules of the game set by the sadistic leaders of the Capitol. Peeta, her fellow tribute from District 12, also provides the more positive influence of this card: stability and a connection to home and humanity in this new chaotic world.

5. The Hierophant - The Hierophant represents tradition, religion, and conformity. The Fool conforms to certain belief systems.

Katniss conforms to the traditions and expectations of the games. President Snow and the Head Gamemaker, Seneca Crane, both serve as Hierophant figures. The career tributes also uphold traditions and conformity to keep the districts in line.

6. THE LOVERS - THE LOVERS REPRESENT RELATIONSHIPS, VALUES, AND CHOICES. THE FOOL EXPERIENCES LOVE AND HAS TO MAKE AN IMPORTANT CHOICE.

During a televised interview before the Games begin, Peeta confesses his feelings for Katniss, hurtling them into the role of star-crossed lovers. Peeta represents values like staying true to oneself and not losing one's humanity even in the face of evil. However, Katniss resists feelings for him. His values are a luxury she cannot afford if she has any chance of making it home to her sister.

Katniss eventually comes to love Peeta and has to choose between saving him and winning the games.

A platonic version of this card's influence is Katniss forming an alliance and kinship with Rue, a young tribute who reminds Katniss of her beloved sister. Katniss chooses to honor Rue and give her a makeshift funeral even though she knows it will upset the gamemakers.

7. THE CHARIOT - THE CHARIOT REPRESENTS OVERCOMING OBSTACLES, PROGRESS, AND WILLPOWER. THE FOOL BEGINS MOVING FORWARD IN A DETERMINED WAY.

Katniss makes progress in the Games, powered by her determination and will to survive and return home.

8. STRENGTH – STRENGTH REPRESENTS COURAGE, BRAVERY, AND INNER STRENGTH. THE FOOL TAPS INTO INNER FORTITUDE AND RESILIENCE TO CONTINUE THE JOURNEY.

Katniss finds her inner courage and strength which allows her to continue fighting in the games. This card can also represent bringing animal instinct and vulnerability into balance. Katniss shows both physical strength and emotional courage when she makes the choices to honor Rue and help Peeta, despite the risks of caring for someone in this impossible situation.

9. THE HERMIT – THE HERMIT REPRESENTS SOLITUDE, INTROSPECTION, AND GUIDANCE. THE FOOL WITHDRAWS TO LOOK INWARD AND GAINS WISDOM AND COUNSEL FOR THE ROAD AHEAD.

After allying and bonding with young tribute Rue, Katniss looks inside herself and questions her strategy.

Later in the story, Katniss has another Hermit moment when she nurses Peeta back to health in the cave and gains the insights that will guide her through the rest of the story.

10. WHEEL OF FORTUNE - THE WHEEL TURNS, REPRESENTING HOW LUCK, OPPORTUNITIES, AND FORTUNE ARE ALWAYS CHANGING IN LIFE. THE FOOL'S LUCK CHANGES FOR BETTER OR WORSE.

Basically, all the plot twists, good and bad, that send Katniss and the game spinning in new directions are Wheel of Fortune Moments. Delivery of a much-needed salve, allying with Rue, the change in rules to allow two victors, the retraction of that rule, etc.

11. JUSTICE - JUSTICE REPRESENTS REASON, RESPONSIBILITY, AND IMPORTANT DECISIONS. THE FOOL GRAPPLES WITH BALANCING JUSTICE, ETHICS, AND REASON.

After Rue's death, Katniss surrounds her with flowers and does her District 11 salute and whistle, an act of defiance against the Capitol. She chooses connection and humanity over the Capitol's ruthless violence for sport. She also vows to avenge Rue's death.

12. THE HANGED MAN - THE HANGED MAN REPRESENTS SACRIFICE, DELAY, AND GIVING UP CONTROL. THE FOOL MUST SURRENDER AND SEE THINGS FROM A NEW PERSPECTIVE.

When Katniss takes an injured Peeta to a cave to tend to his wounds, their time together forces Katniss to see things from his perspective. She must sacrifice her drive to play on the offensive and close up emotionally. During this time of delay when she has little control, she begins to question her drive to get back to her sister at all costs.

13. DEATH - DEATH REPRESENTS ENDINGS, TRANSITIONS, AND ELIMINATIONS OF THINGS THAT ARE NO LONGER SERVING THE FOOL. THE FOOL EXPERIENCES A SYMBOLIC DEATH OF SOMETHING IMPORTANT.

After her time with Rue and Peeta, Katniss realizes the value of Peeta's ideals. Her previous drive to work within the rigid rules of an unjust system to get home to her family no longer serves her. She begins to push back against the oppressive system to fight for the people she loves.

14. TEMPERANCE - TEMPERANCE REPRESENTS BALANCE, MODERATION, AND PATIENCE. THE FOOL REGAINS EQUILIBRIUM AND HARMONY.

Katniss and Peeta experience a time of harmony when they work together and care for one another.

15. THE DEVIL - THE DEVIL REPRESENTS BONDAGE, ADDICTION, AND GIVING INTO TEMPTATION OR UNHEALTHY ASPECTS OF LIFE. THE FOOL CONFRONTS DARKNESS AND HAS TO FREE THEMSELVES FROM RESTRAINTS.

Even with Katniss's evolving perspective, she still wrestles with her deep-seated drive to survive for her sister. It's easier to fall in line and play the Capitol's games without resisting, but she's no longer sure she can live with herself if she does.

16. THE TOWER - THE TOWER REPRESENTS DISRUPTION, CHANGE, AND AWAKENING. THE FOOL'S EXISTING STRUCTURES IN LIFE CRUMBLE AWAY, BUILT ON SHAKY FOUNDATIONS.

When only a few contestants remain, all are called back to the cornucopia, throwing everything into chaos again.

17. THE STAR - THE STAR BRINGS RENEWED HOPE, INSPIRATION, AND PURPOSE. THE FOOL STARTS TO FEEL OPTIMISTIC AGAIN ABOUT THE JOURNEY.

The gamemakers announce a rule change that allows two victors from the same district. Katniss lets hope bloom and renews her determination to bring Peeta home.

18. THE MOON - THE MOON REPRESENTS FEARS, ILLUSIONS, AND THE SUBCONSCIOUS. THE FOOL FEELS LOST, EXPERIENCES SELF-DOUBTS, AND ENCOUNTERS HIDDEN ENEMIES.

The gamemakers strike another cruel blow. When only Katniss and Peeta remain, they retract their rule change. Katniss must now kill or be killed to end the game. All Katniss's fears converge as she and Peeta face an impossible situation.

19. THE SUN - THE SUN BRINGS NEW JOY, ENLIGHTENMENT, AND SUCCESS. THE FOOL EMERGES FROM DARKNESS INTO LIGHT, GAINING CLARITY AND NEW ENERGY.

Katniss and Peeta decide to defy the gamemakers' sadistic imperative to kill each other. Before they can eat poison berries as a final act of defiance, they are both declared victors and transported out of the arena.

20. JUDGMENT - JUDGMENT REPRESENTS REFLECTION, RECKONING, AND AWAKENING TO A CALLING. THE FOOL EVALUATES THEIR PROGRESS AND IS CALLED TO A HIGHER PURPOSE.

After the games end, Katniss and Peeta are both alive and able to return to their families. They won by refusing to let the Capitol take their humanity. The seeds of rebellion have been planted for Katniss to be called to a higher purpose of defying the Capitol in later books.

Seneca Crane, the head gamemaker gets a reckoning of his own when President Snow renews his resolve to quash all disobedience and ruthlessly eliminate all who defy him or don't fall in line.

21. THE WORLD –THE WORLD REPRESENTS COMPLETION, FULFILLMENT, AND WHOLENESS. THE FOOL'S JOURNEY COMES FULL CIRCLE, WITH THE FOOL FINDING MEANING AND PURPOSE.

After Katniss and Peeta are crowned victors of the Hunger Games, their defiance and romantic storyline stir hope for change among the districts and cast doubt on the Capitol's power.

An outraged President Snow threatens Katniss and her family to extinguish sparks of rebellion, setting up a whole new cycle of the Fool's Journey for the sequels.

EXERCISE

CHOOSE A BOOK OR MOVIE YOU KNOW WELL. MAP THE STORY'S EVENTS AND ELEMENTS ONTO THE FOOL'S JOURNEY.

USING TAROT ARCHETYPES TO GET INSIDE YOUR CHARACTERS' HEADS

Archetypes are simply patterns that repeat over time. There are many sub-domains of archetypes, such as the character and story beat archetypes, as well as thematic and symbolic archetypes. We saw examples of the former in the Fool's Journey section. Several others you might recognize are the Hero, the Sage, the Trickster, the Seductress, and the Rogue. Even tropes (enemies to lovers, the band of misfits vs. a monster, the chosen one) and genre expectations (tragedies end tragically, romances end with a happily ever after, protagonists do not die) are forms of repeating patterns that fit into the realm of archetypes. These repeating patterns give readers a sense of familiarity and recognition.

However, for storytelling purposes in connection to the tarot, I'm going to focus on four primary **psychological facet archetypes**. Many books for writers cover character archetypes and delve into their templates for repeating patterns of behavior.

Character archetypes focus on what is the **same** across characters. While this is also useful for developing your cast, we're going to zoom in on a sub-domain of archetypes that can help you **differentiate** your characters and make them feel like flawed, realistic individuals whose struggles resonate with your readers.

Your protagonist may still fit into a character archetype. This is not a bad thing. These patterns repeat for a reason, after all. However, by going further and exploring aspects of your character's psyche, you can build on one of those character templates that speaks to readers. For your audience, this delivers the comfort of familiar patterns, **plus** the surprise and delight of discovering your unique nuanced spin. Double win.

INTO THE MIND OF YOUR CHARACTERS

We're going to look at four facets of the human mind that can help us dig deeper into the inner workings of your cast. Examining these facets of our characters helps us understand and convey how they see themselves, what mask they present to the world, what traits they'd rather hide, and how they don't quite fit societal expectations. Each of these aspects can help you ramp up the tension and emotional resonance of your characters and plot.

So, what are they? Jung identified four key archetypes that relate to facets of the human psyche: The Persona, The Shadow, The Anima and Animus, and The Self.

Next, we'll analyze each of these archetypes, followed by examples of how various tarot cards could apply to each.

THE PERSONA

The Persona is the mask or image that we present to the world, designed to make a specific impression on others while concealing anything in our nature that we view as taboo or not in alignment with who we aspire to be.

I mentioned earlier in the book that we often compare our messy insides to other people's polished and curated outsides. Those Instagram-ready outsides are the carefully constructed personas that those people choose to show the world. While the persona might be an authentic facet of this person's world, it's never the entire picture. Upholding this flawless facade is often motivated by insecurities, fear, self-preservation, or the weight of expectations.

People may adopt personas that help them feel powerful, rich, intelligent, trustworthy, kind and nurturing, supportive, in charge, independent, high-status, high-achieving, "normal," protected, or like they have it all-together.

How can we use our character's Persona(s) to deepen our stories?

There's always a great deal of tension between how people want to be seen and the whole picture behind the scenes.

I've got news for you: nobody has it all together. Even if they look like they do.

The kind of persona a character projects clues us in on what they view as valuable or what they aspire to be. Personas also speak to the values of the society characters live in, the groups they belong to, etc. They give away what the character understands to be acceptable or unacceptable, valued or taboo in the story context. At the scene level, you can contrast the persona a character presents (their outward actions, dialogue, and manner) with their inner monologue or subtext. Using this technique effectively showcases the character's feelings of not belonging, as well as any insecurities or irritations they may have regarding the expectations placed upon them.

This approach also does double duty: providing character insight and world-building in a way that shows rather than tells the audience the rules of the story world.

Another way we can put personas to work in a story is to remember that many people will go to extravagant lengths to uphold their public personas. Think about what a character might do to avoid knowledge of their shadow side getting out.

THE SHADOW

The Shadow is the darker, more primal part of our personality. It's the place inside where we hide the traits we repress, along with our weaknesses, shortcomings, and baser instincts that would not be acceptable in polite society.

Though some aspects one hides in the shadow may be unethical or illegal, not all shadow traits are inherently bad. A more useful way to think of them is as the parts that don't align with the image a character wants to project. For example, a character who is running for mayor on a platform of family values will probably try to hide his marital indiscretions and that he curses like a sailor while watching hockey games. A character on a job interview might downplay or hide their troubles with time management or organization.

Some examples of traits a character might push into the shadow and deny are weakness, laziness, taboo sexual proclivities, impulses to hurt others or worse, imperfections, a desire to be wild and free, ambition, greed, disregard for others, fears, political interests, prejudice, humble upbringing, unsavory characters in their family lineage, or use of company funds for personal gain.

HOW CAN WE USE OUR CHARACTER'S SHADOW(S) TO DEEPEN OUR STORIES?

Behind every persona is a shadow. Giving readers a glimpse of traits that your character denies or hides can make them more human and relatable.

Sometimes a reader may share that shadow trait, and reading about it is a much healthier way to acknowledge and explore this trait than to act on it in the real world.

Also, the interplay between a character's shadow and persona can add complexity that makes the character more resonant. Even if the reader and the character have nothing in common on the surface, every human has wrestled with warring aspects of themselves. Most of us yearn to belong, to be valued and accepted. Sometimes, this means crafting a persona and molding ourselves into what society, family, or a particular group holds up as the ideal.

But fitting in is not the same as truly belonging. What do we do when parts of ourselves don't fit that ideal? It's risky, in some cases, a matter of life and death, to shine a light on those facets. At the same time, it can also be caustic and soul-crushing to hide them. This is a universal struggle we can gift to our characters. Readers can relate to this on a visceral level, and when that happens, you create emotional investment. This tension also adds a layer of conflict and personal stakes to stories.

THE ANIMA AND ANIMUS

The Anima represents the feminine aspects present in the male collective unconscious, and Animus represents the masculine aspects present in women's collective unconscious.

To put this in terms that might apply to character creation, the Anima and Animus deal with society's ideas about "masculine" and "feminine" behavior, including the social norms for what is acceptable inside of these gender roles and wrestling with the duality of behaviors, impulses, traits, and desires that fall outside of that binary.[1]

HOW CAN WE USE THE ANIMA OR ANIMUS TO DEEPEN OUR STORIES?

Much like Shadow traits, grappling with the Anima or Animus can give an extra dimension to our characters. Feeling like we don't quite fit in is another universal experience. Showing areas in which our characters feel like outsiders can also forge a bond with the reader.

THE SELF

The Self archetype represents the unified consciousness and unconsciousness of an individual. The creation of the Self occurs through individuation, where an individual integrates various aspects of their personality.

This archetype is what we see in a guru or wise mentor character or when a protagonist reaches the end of their character arc. They have learned their lessons, faced their demons (sometimes literal *and* figurative), shed remnants of their old selves, and can now integrate the wisdom they've gained through the experience.

HOW CAN WE USE THE SELF TO DEEPEN OUR STORIES?

Ask yourself, what does the self-actualized version of your character look like? Make sure they're not already there at the beginning of the story. Stories are much more satisfying when we're mean to our characters and make them work for it. You can also think about what your character's like at the beginning of the story and what challenges could catalyze the lessons and growth needed to become the best version of themselves.

EXERCISE

IF YOU'RE WRESTLING WITH A ONE-DIMENSIONAL CHARACTER, CONSIDER WHAT EACH OF THESE ARCHETYPES MIGHT LOOK LIKE FOR THAT INDIVIDUAL.

Ask yourself:

1. What is my character's **persona**? What is the image they project to the world?

2. What is in my character's **shadow**? What is this character ashamed of? What parts do they keep hidden to keep that perfect persona image in place

3. What does your character have in their **Anima** or **Animus**? Another way to think of this question, considering a broader gender spectrum, is: what are some dualities or contradictions in the way your character behaves versus how society expects them to behave?4. What might an evolved version, **aka the Self**, of your character look like? What trials would they have to face to grow and gain the courage to integrate parts of themselves that they want to hide away?

ARCHETYPES IN ACTION

Let's say you wanted to pull tarot cards to explore ideas about a character's Persona, Shadow, Anima, or Animus, or what their evolved Self would look like.

Below are examples of how selected tarot cards might be interpreted in terms of these archetypes of the psyche.

THE PERSONA

The Sun: An outward presentation of cheery positivity, vitality, confidence, and success. Someone with a Sun persona might project an image of unflappability and live by the mantra that happiness is a choice.

The Chariot: The Chariot exudes victory, control, and unwavering determination. Someone with a Chariot persona might be an elite athlete, surgeon, politician, or billionaire who wants to be seen as driven, and always victorious, able to control their environment and do whatever it takes to succeed.

The High Priestess: Someone with a High Priestess persona may cultivate an air of mystery or appear aloof or calculated on the outside, choosing to conceal or reveal their intuitive nature and hidden parts of themselves only when they choose. Think of a character like Elsa from *Frozen*.

The Shadow

The Devil: The Devil card represents the addictions and the vices we chain ourselves to. If the Devil card represents your character's shadow, they probably have an addiction or vice they want to hide from others in the story. Some addictions can be taboo, illegal, or socially unacceptable, while others might be put in the Shadow because they don't align with the Persona we wish to present to the world. Examples could be alcohol, drugs, vanity, sex, overwork, extreme control over food intake, and people-pleasing at the cost of our well-being.

The Moon: The Moon can represent fear, uncertainty, and the murkier aspects of the unconscious mind. Some shadow traits we repress so thoroughly that they hide in wait from our conscious minds and the outside world. If the Moon represents your character's Shadow, they might want to hide any fear or uncertainty they feel or that they rely on intuition when they'd rather be seen as logical.

Eight of Cups: The Eight of Cups represents withdrawal, retreat, recognizing sunk costs, and letting go. Pulling the Eight of Cups as a character's Shadow card might indicate a tendency to abandon situations when things get tough rather than face the hard emotional truths necessary to work through conflict. A character with an Eight of Cups shadow might leave a trail of unresolved issues or be someone who cuts and runs before someone can leave them.

Ten of Swords: Ten of Swords represents painful conclusions, betrayal, downfall, and hitting rock bottom. A Ten of Swords Shadow might present as a martyr complex or a victim mentality. With this card's indications of betrayal and defeat, a Ten of Swords shadow could also look like giving up too easily when defeated, always returning to the safety net rather than facing the consequences of avoiding uncomfortable truths that led them down this path in the first place.

The Anima and Animus

Though the traditional ideas of the Anima and Animus deal with masculine traits in the feminine psyche and feminine traits in the masculine psyche, I've adopted a slightly different take for storytelling purposes. As you'll see in some of the following examples, I've considered any gender-based traits or norms that create cognitive dissonance for a character.

Anima: Feminine Aspects

The Empress: The Empress persona is one of nurturing and growth. A person might identify as female but feel ambivalent or even repelled by the expectation to nurture and have children. In contrast, a man or non-binary individual may feel a deep call to nurture and raise children.

Queen Cards: Queens of each suit evoke different aspects of feminine energy, from fiery passion (Wands), intuition and nurturing (Cups), cunning, intellect, or logic (Swords), or grounded, practical, and resourceful (Pentacles). If one of these appears as your character's Anima, they may feel dissonance or discomfort about possessing this trait.

Animus: Masculine Aspects

The Emperor: The Emperor represents the traditional masculine ideal of structure, authority, and control. An individual who identifies as male may feel stifled by the prospect of taking over the mantle of leadership of his family business and prefer a profession with less authority where he can make a social impact, like teaching, or one that affords more freedom to pursue art or spend time with his family. If you pull an Emperor card to represent a woman's Animus, she may be an authority figure or someone who naturally exerts control over others and may feel anger or discomfort over the push back she gets for doing so.

King Cards: Kings of each suit symbolize different aspects of masculine energy: passionate, visionary leadership, drive to explore and conquer (Wands), maturity in handling relationships and interpersonal communication (Cups—note: the King of Cups exhibits the most balance between the masculine and feminine parts of the psyche), clarity of thought, decision-making and leadership based on impartiality and insight (Swords), and pragmatic, reliable, adept at managing practical matters, driven to provide stability and security (Pentacles). If one of these appears as your character's Animus, they may feel dissonance or discomfort about possessing this trait.

THE SELF

The World: The World card represents the culmination of a cycle and an integration of both the conscious aspects (Personas)and the unconscious aspects (the Shadow and Anima or Animus) of the Self to become whole.

Judgment: The penultimate card in the Major Arcana also speaks to self-evaluation, forgiveness, and rebirth into a life more in line with one's true, more complete Self.

***These are just a few examples. Let's dive into more about how to use the cards in your writing practice.

---

1. . Jung, of course, lived in a time before the idea of a gender spectrum outside that binary was acknowledged.

PART FOUR

GETTING STARTED WITH THE TAROT

STEP-BY-STEP INSTRUCTIONS

WHAT YOU'LL NEED TO GET STARTED

Now the real fun begins. The exercises and prompts in the following chapters can be used to tackle nearly any aspect of your story.

HERE'S WHAT YOU'LL NEED FOR THESE TAROT PROMPTING EXERCISES:

- A story question to work with

- A deck of tarot cards

- At least 10 minutes (30+ minutes allows for deeper reflection)

- A notebook or somewhere to jot down your impressions and reflections

TAROT DECKS

In addition to your story question, you'll need a tarot deck to make the most of these exercises. You can find tarot decks in many places, such as your local indie bookstore, online retailers, and even eBay. If luxe artisan-crafted decks are your speed, check out Kickstarter and Etsy.

If you're waiting for your deck to arrive, or you find yourself out and about with time for an impromptu tarot session, try an online tarot randomizer like the one at https://randomtarotcard.com/. This is also a great resource if you want to try out these exercises and see if they're a good fit for you before investing in a deck.

However, for prompts that require drawing multiple cards, I suggest working with an actual deck whenever possible. You can only choose one card at a time with the randomizer, and it will disappear when you move on to later cards.

CHOOSING YOUR DECK

When choosing a deck to help with your writing, here are some factors to consider:

The Mood or Vibe of the Cards

Look for decks with imagery that creates a mood that resonates with you. Think of what could work with the tone and feel of the genre(s) you write. I might use a more playful deck like the Cute Ghost Tarot for a cozy mystery plot but gravitate toward The Dark Wood or the Tarot of the Haunted House for something with more ominous elements. The traditional Rider-Waite-Smith deck has a more neutral mood and is, therefore, more versatile if you want to stick to a single deck. Some find its aesthetic old-fashioned for their taste, but there are also great contemporary decks like The Modern Witch Tarot Deck by Lisa Sterle that draw on Pamela Colman Smith's symbol-rich imagery with an updated design style.

Art Style

When looking at decks, pay attention to which art styles appeal to you and bring you joy when you look at them. My friend Sarah says one of the things she likes about using tarot decks for writing is the bonus of having a pocketful of beautiful art.

Complexity of Illustrations

If possible, look at a selection of the individual cards in a deck. This might not be an option at retailers, but if a deck catches your eye, search YouTube for a tarot deck flip through or an unboxing video.

Are the illustrations spare and minimalist? Though this style might suit other purposes, the more richly detailed the cards are, the more input you'll have to work with when using tarot for brainstorming ideas.

Branded Decks

It might be tempting to grab a deck featuring your favorite demon-hunting brothers from Supernatural, the Golden Girls, or your favorite animated villains. That's totally fine if those speak to you, but keep in mind that you'll have pre-existing associations with the characters and images on the cards. This may help you reinforce genre tropes, but it may also limit your interpretations to more familiar categories and impressions. This could also reduce the randomness factor and thus the effectiveness in subverting the efficiency principle because of your familiarity with the people and places on the cards.

Personally, I like to switch things up and cycle through different decks. If you only have one deck, consider organizing a swap with writer friends who also use tarot prompts. Alternatively, pull cards from your own deck and find flip-through videos of unfamiliar decks on YouTube to interpret the corresponding cards.

Working with a variety of decks makes my ADHD brain happy and keeps the novelty from wearing off.

Some of my favorite decks are:

- **The Dark Wood Tarot:** This one has a spooky vibe, and the illustrations create a gorgeous, deliciously dark and dangerous fairytale woods atmosphere. Sasha Graham, the author of this deck, is a gifted storyteller, and reading her card interpretations in the guidebook feels like a journey through the dark woods.

- **The Light Seers Tarot:** This deck has a sense of exuberance and a Zen vibe, with a bright, joyful color palette and feel to the cards. The artist also depicts a range of ethnicities on the cards.

- **Tarot of the Haunted House:** With artwork and a mood inspired by the covers of 60s and 70s gothic novels, this collaboration between Sasha Graham and artist Mirco Pierfederici recreates the gothic haunted house vibe. Many of the visuals are unexpected with great twists on traditional imagery and interpretations. The whole deck has a strong story-telling point of view.

- **The Modern Witch Tarot:** This deck by illustrator Lisa Serle has a modern, witchy, feminist vibe. I love the artist's bold use of color and diverse range of ethnicities and gender presentations on the cards in positions of power.

- **Cirque du Tarot:** This deck has a whimsical, enchanted circus vibe, with vibrant, almost glowing colors that add to the spectacle. The dreamy imagery sets the stage for a magical scene. The guidebook, authored by Leeza Robertson, is one of my favorites. It employs drama and stagecraft to interpret the cards in unique ways.

- **The Cute Ghost Tarot:** Though not for everyone, this playful deck has a lighthearted, quirky vibe that matches the tone of my paranormal cozy mysteries. It features adorable cartoon ghost takes on traditional Rider Waite Smith imagery. The Devil card makes me laugh out loud every time I see it.

Chapter 4.2
Step-by-Step Process

Stages Where Prompting May Be Helpful

Brainstorming and Pre-writing:
Use tarot prompts in the pre-writing phase to flesh out seeds of ideas, develop your characters, their allies, and enemies, round out your suspect list, or plan your plot.

In Medias Res: In the thick of writing, grab a deck and a prompt anytime you hit an impasse, get stuck, bored, or need an unexpected idea.

Revision: Deploy the exercises in the revision process to deepen characters, character arcs, relationships and themes. You can also use the cards to strengthen plots and pacing.

Tarot Prompting: A Step-by-Step Process

The Tarot Prompting Process works like this:

Step 1

First, find a quiet spot where you can concentrate.

STEP 2

Spend a few minutes thinking or journaling about the story question you'd like to work on. You can also do this in advance while driving, in the shower, etc. What do you already know? What puzzle piece(s) are you missing?

STEP 3

Based on what came up in step 2, choose a prompt to help you go deeper into what you need ideas for. (Look for the Prompt Library in the next section: Part 5). You can also create your own prompt.

For easier navigation, the Prompt Library in this book is divided into the following sections:

- Character and Relationship Prompts

- Plot, Setting, and Worldbuilding Prompts

- Prompts to Get You Unstuck

STEP 4

Grab a tarot deck.

Shuffle with your scene question(s) in mind.

STEP 5

When you feel ready, draw one to three cards (or the number of cards suggested for your chosen prompt) and interpret them for your answers.

Note that there is no one "right" way to shuffle or choose which cards you draw. If you prefer to let your intuition guide you, go for it. If that doesn't feel comfortable, some alternatives are to set a timer as you shuffle or wait until you're done thinking through the problem.

As for choosing which cards to draw, there are several methods:

- Choose cards from the top of the deck.

- Cut the deck then choose cards from the top.

- Fan out the cards and choose at random, or let your intuition guide you.

STEP 6

Once you've chosen your cards, jump to Part 7 of this book for instructions on how to interpret them for story ideas.

Part Five

Tarot Prompt Library

CHAPTER 5.1
CHARACTER AND RELATIONSHIP PROMPTS

CHARACTER PROMPTS

- **Back story**: What events from your character's past shape who they are today? Draw three cards for insight.

- **Wound**: What traumatic event from your character's past keeps them stuck, protecting them from harm but also from growth and fully living? Draw one card for the event, one card for how they are stuck, one for how staying stuck protects them, and one for what dream lies beyond that stuck place.

- **Driven**: What drives your character? Why do they want to solve this crime, open this bakery, discover life on a new planet, win the heart of the person they love, etc? Draw one to three cards.

- **Goal**: What's your character's goal in this story? Why is it important? What happens if they don't meet the goal? Draw one card for each question.

- **Essence**: What traits embody the essential facets of your character? Draw one to three cards.

- **Persona**: Draw one card representing the public persona or mask your character projects to the world around them. What does this persona reveal about their values and priorities? Draw another card to symbolize what this mask suggests the character believes society expects of them.

- **Shadow:** What aspects of themselves does your character push into their shadow? Draw one to three cards.

- **Anima and Animus**: What traditionally feminine or masculine traits does your character have that don't align with their society's prescribed gender norms? Draw one to three cards.

- **Surprising detail**: What's a surprising detail you could add to your character's personality? Draw one card.

- **Secret**: What's your character hiding? Why? What would happen if someone revealed their secret? Draw one card for each of these questions.

- **Stakes**: What's at stake if your character cannot achieve their goal? Draw one to three cards.

- **Stuck**: What keeps your character stuck? Why? What are the consequences of remaining stuck?

- **Growth**: What does your character need to grow or change into the person they aspire to be? What kind of character could challenge your character to spur change? What events could catalyze this change? Draw one card for each question.

- **The Dark Side**: If you have a character that feels too perfect or overly bright and cheery, what's on their dark side? Draw one to three cards.

- **The Bright Side**: If you have a character that feels too perfectly evil, what's on their bright side? Draw one to three cards.

- **Blind Spot**: Who or what is your character's blind spot? Why? How does this blind spot complicate story events? Draw one card for each question.

- **Obstacles: Big, Bigger, Biggest: Part 1:** What obstacles of increasing intensity can you throw in your character's path to their goal? Draw one card for each obstacle.

- **Obstacles: Big, Bigger, Biggest: Part 2: Make it Personal**: Complete your spread for Big, Bigger, Biggest: Part 1 as instructed. Next, how can each obstacle become more personal for your character? For example, if obstacle 3 is that if your character gets distracted and misses apprehending the killer, you can add a more personal dimension if they've recently been reprimanded, or beat themselves up about getting distracted. Alternately, they might lose out on the big promotion opportunity that could pay their twins' college tuition, or disappoint their spouse, who has already started looking at new houses that they'll never be able to afford if the promotion falls through. Draw one card for each obstacle.

- **False Belief**: What false belief does your character wrestle with? How does this belief affect their life? Draw one card for the false belief. Draw two more for the impacts.

- **Outer Expectations**: What expectations do others place on your protagonist? Draw one to three cards.

- **Inner Expectations**: What does your protagonist expect of themselves? Why? Draw three cards for insight.

- **The Weight of Expectations**: What outside expectations does your protagonist resent or chafe at? Why? Draw three cards.

- **Hopes and Fears**: What does your character hope for? What do they fear? Draw one card to represent each.

- **Alignment:** What's out of alignment for your character? What are the effects of this misalignment? What needs to change for your character to get back into alignment? Draw one card for each question.

- **Anti-Hero**: In what ways does your character create problems for themselves? What are the story consequences? Draw three cards to represent the problems. Draw three more for impacts on the story.

- **Swiss Army Knife**: What special skills, competencies, or resources does your character have that help them overcome obstacles? Draw three cards.

- **Puppet**: If your character feels controlled by someone else in the story, who's pulling the strings? In what ways? Draw one card to represent the controlling force. Draw two cards for insight into the motivation behind and effects of this control.

- **Light**: What lights your character up? Draw one card.

- **Play**: What does play look like for your character? What hobbies or leisure activities does your character engage in? Draw one to three cards.

- **Unpopular Opinion**: What unpopular opinion does your character hold? Draw one to three cards for insight.

- **Three Wishes**: If your character had three wishes, what would they be? Draw three cards. Choose one you could feature in your story. Draw another card to show the effects this longing has on story events.

- **Be Careful What You Wish For**: What does your character want? If they got this, how could it go spectacularly wrong and create problems? Draw one card for the wish, one to illuminate how it could go wrong.

- **Projection**: What trait does your character criticize in others because deep down, it's a trait they dislike in themselves or wish they had the courage to act on? Draw one card.

- **Et Tu Brute?**: Who or what does your character feel betrayed by? How does that shape them? Draw one card to represent the backstabber. Draw two to three cards for effects of the betrayal.

- **The Toddler Approach**: To explore the deeper motivations behind a key decision your character is making, follow these steps:

  - Identify the decision you want to analyze. Ask yourself "Why would they make that decision?" and draw a card. Dig deeper by asking "Why?" again and drawing another card to build on the previous card's meaning. Repeat drawing additional "Why?" cards as needed to peel back layers of your character's motivations.

- **Audience Connector**: What actions can the protagonist take that will connect with the reader? Blake Snyder calls this a "save the cat" moment. Draw one to three cards for inspiration.

- **Midnights**: What keeps your character up at night? Draw one to three cards.

- **Fate**: What are your character's thoughts on destiny? How does this affect their choices in the story? Draw one card for their attitude and one to three to show how it affects their decision-making.

- **Tell → Show: Character Traits**: Think of a trait or aspect you want to convey about your character. Draw one to three cards for inspiration to take this from abstract to concrete. For example: If I wanted to show a character was great at schmoozing and I drew the Three of cups, I might write a scene in which I show her at a business dinner enjoying drinks and conversation with colleagues.

- **Tell → Show: Mood or Emotional State**: Think of a mood or emotional state you want to convey. Draw three cards for inspiration on how to take this from abstract to concrete. For example, if my protagonist was worried about something, and I drew the Eight of Pentacles, I might show them throwing themselves into work to avoid the problem or accidentally messing up something really important at work because their mind wandered.

- **The High Priestess:** Since the Priestess is all about duality, what two aspects or opposing forces need to be brought into balance within your character? Draw two cards.

- **Skeletons in the Closet**: What's your character hiding? Draw one to three cards to illuminate their secrets.

- **Spill the Tea**: If your character were featured in a gossip column, what would it be for? Draw one to three cards.

- **Rip Van Winkle**: Imagine your character fell asleep for 20 years. What would they miss most? Draw one to three cards.

- **Insight**: What unique insight or perspective does your character bring to the story problem? How did they come by this insight? How does it show up in the story? Draw a card for each question.

- **Sage**: Who does your character view as wise? How can you incorporate this person into your story? Draw one card for each question.

- **Insecure**: What does your character feel insecure about? Are the insecurities warranted? Draw one card to answer each question.

- **Anonymous**: What would your character secretly like to do if they could be anonymous? How could you use this knowledge in your story? Draw a card for each question.

- **SWOT Analysis**: Do a SWOT analysis for your character. In business planning, this type of analysis is done to think through a business's strengths, weaknesses, opportunities, and threats. Draw four cards, one for your character's strength, one for their weakness, one for an opportunity, and the last for a threat.

- **SWOT Analysis for Your Character's Business**: If starting, taking over, or keeping a business open is part of your character's story, follow the steps in the previous prompt with your character's business in mind.

- **Character Bio: Clues from a Single Card**: What aspects of your character and their background and day-to-day life do you need to figure out? Choose one or more aspect to focus on.

  a. Variant 1: Choose one card during a session: Choose an aspect to focus on (for example: work, weird talents, or how they feel about their appearance). Draw one to three cards for insight into that area of their life.

  b. Variant 2: Choose multiple cards during a session: Decide on a character and multiple aspects of that character to flesh out the person as a whole. Grab some sticky notes or index cards and write each aspect you want to explore. Draw a card and lay it on top of each aspect you've written down.

- Here are some ideas for character traits or background info you might use for this spread:

  ○ What's your character's personality like?

  ○ What are your character's strengths?

  ○ What are your character's flaws?

  ○ What are your character's areas of competence?

  ○ What are your character's areas of incompetence?

- What archetypal personality fits your character?

- What are your character's aspirations that they share with the world?

- What are your character's private aspirations?

- What does your character like about themselves?

- What does your character wish they could change about themselves?

- What's your character's favorite season?

- What's your character's personal style?

- What's your character's obsession?

- What are your character's pet peeves?

- Is your character compliant or rebellious?

- What's your character's occupation?

- What's your character's relationship with their boss and coworkers like?

- How does your character feel about their occupation? Is it something they fell into or planned?

- Who does your character feel closest to?

- Is your character an introvert or extrovert?

- Is your character passive, assertive, or aggressive?

- It's Friday night. What's your character doing?

- Superlative: If your character was voted "Most likely to _______," how would people fill in the blank?

- What's your character's space like at home?

- What's your character's space like at work?

- What's your character's social life like?

- What's your character's biggest fear?

- What makes your character angry? Why?

- What is your character's defense mechanism?

- How does your character react to conflict?

- Is your character an optimist or a pessimist?

- What's something about your character that annoys others?

- What's something about your character that charms others?

- How does your character feel about authority?

- How adventurous is your character?

- What's your character's socio-economic status?

- Does your character have siblings? What are their sibling relationships like?

- What's your character's relationship with their family like?

- If there was a family rift, what caused it?

- What did your character do well as a kid?

- What did your character do badly as a kid?

- What's your character's attitude about romantic relationships?

- Is your character in a relationship now? How's that going?

- What are your character's unhealthy habits?

- How does your character deal with stress?

- **Your Character's Enneagram Number**: Separate one full suit of Minor Arcana from your deck (Wands, Cups, Swords or Pentacles). Choose a suit at random or pick one that feels most fitting for your character. Set aside the court cards and the Ten card. Shuffle cards Ace (One) through Nine only. Draw one card for each character. Note the number on the card. Find the corresponding Enneagram Type below and look up the traits associated with that type to add nuance to your character's personality.

  - Type One: The Reformer

  - Type Two: The Helper

  - Type Three: The Achiever

  - Type Four: The Individualist

  - Type Five: The Investigator

  - Type Six: They Loyalist

  - Type Seven: The Enthusiast

  - Type Eight: The Challenger

  - Type Nine: The Peacemaker

- **Two Truths and a Lie**: Play the Two Truths and a Lie game for the character you're exploring. In this icebreaker game, a person presents three statements about themselves to a group. The group must guess which two statements are facts and which is a fabrication. To do this, choose a character to work with. Draw three cards. Imagine a story from your character's past inspired by each card. Make two of them true and one a lie.

CHARACTER ARCS

- **Guilt**: What guilt does your character need to release in order to grow? Draw one to three cards.

- **Forgiveness**: Does your character need to forgive someone? Who? Draw one to three cards for insights.

- **Setbacks**: What setbacks can your protagonist face on the way to the changes they need to make in their life? Draw three cards.

- **The Past, The Present, The Future**: Draw cards to give insight into your character's past, present, and future.

CHARACTER RELATIONSHIP DYNAMICS PROMPTS

- **Light up my Life**: Choose two characters. Draw cards for each of the following questions:

  - What lights character A up? Draw one card.

  - What lights character B up? Draw one card.

  - How can you use this knowledge to deepen the bond between the characters? Draw one to three cards.

- **Found Family**: Who makes up your character's found family? What connects each with your protagonist? What tension exists between them?

- ○ **Version 1:** Decide how many characters you'll focus on. Draw one card to represent each character and their personality. Directly below each character card, draw a second card that represents their connection to the protagonist. Draw a third card for each that represents tension or conflict between this character and the protagonist.

- ○ **Version 2:** You can use this one if you've already developed the personalities of your supporting cast. Choose the characters you will work with. For each one, draw a card that represents their connection to the protagonist. Draw a second card for each that represents tension or conflict between this character and the protagonist.

- **Band of Misfits**: If your story includes a group of characters that come together based on their shared outsider experience (think the Losers Club from Stephen King's *It*), this is a spread for you. First, decide how many characters to work with. Draw a card to represent each character's personality or chief interest. For each character, draw a second card to illuminate why or how they're an outsider. Draw a third card to represent how each character was pulled into your protagonist's world.

- **Cheerleaders**: Who are your character's biggest supporters? Draw one card to represent each person. Draw a second card to illuminate how they show up for the protagonist.

- **Naysayers**: Who are your character's biggest detractors? Draw one card to represent each person. Draw a second card to show why they dislike or antagonize the protagonist.

- **It's Complicated**: What relationship does your protagonist have that creates conflicts in reaching their goals? Draw one card to represent the relationship that creates conflict. Draw two cards to illustrate how that relationship causes conflicts. Draw two more cards to illustrate why the relationship is still important, anyway.

- **Social Distortion**: What social conflicts does your character face in this story? How does that affect your protagonist's ability to reach their goals? Draw one card for the conflict and three cards for insight into effects on goals.

- **Workplace Drama**: What workplace conflict plagues your character in this story? How does it affect your protagonist's ability to reach their goals? Draw one card for the conflict and three for insight into effects on their goals.

- **Tell → Show**: **Tension between Two Characters**: Think of a point in your story where tension is high between two characters. Draw one to three cards for inspiration on how to take this tension from abstract to concrete. For example, if I wanted to convey that my protagonist and her friend are feeling pitted against one another, and I drew the Six of Wands, I might write a scene showing one of the character is celebrated and honored while the other one is overlooked, causing tension in the relationship.

- **Using Setting to Amplify Relationship Conflict**: Find a point in your story where tension simmers between two characters. Draw a card to find a setting that heightens the conflict. Draw a second card to illustrate how that plays out. For instance, in a romance with an income gap between the leads, insecurities arise in one character. If I drew the Four of Wands, I might set a scene at the grand opening of a theater funded by one character's wealthy parents. This emphasizes the disparity, as the other character's parents live paycheck-to-paycheck, driving the conflict further.

- **Push and Pull:** What forces unite and divide your characters? Choose two characters, such as the protagonist and antagonist, colleagues, or romantic interests.

    a. Draw one card for Character A and another for Character B, placing them on opposite sides of your workspace.

    b. Pull: Next, draw two cards representing shared connections between them (interests, family, values, etc.) and place them between the character cards.

    c. Push: Then, draw two cards symbolizing factors that cause conflict or opposition between them, and place those below the connection cards, in the middle.

- This exercise visually maps the dynamics pulling the characters together and pushing them apart.

- **Power Struggles**: Choose two characters locked in a power struggle. Draw one card representing how Character A holds power over Character B. Draw another card for how Character B wields power over Character A. Then, draw two more cards depicting the potential effects of these power dynamics on your work-in-progress.

- **Foils**: In storytelling, a foil is a character who contrasts with another, usually to highlight the differences in the protagonist's character and struggles. For example, in the 1996 movie *Jerry Maguire*, sports agent Jerry inspires others with his ardent idealism in his business decisions, but falls short of that passionate fervor in personal relationships. In contrast, his only client, football player Rod Tidwell, has deeply loving personal relationships, but his attitude and hotheadedness on and around the field leads others to view him as difficult or arrogant. Each highlights what the other is missing and helps the other grow.

    ○ Select two key characters who can act as foils to each other. Draw cards representing each character. Then draw one card for the strength/skill that Character A possesses, but Character B lacks. Draw another card for the strength/skill that Character B has, but Character A needs to learn. This exercise highlights their contrasting qualities.

- **The Usual Suspects**: To develop a list of suspects for a crime in your story, follow these steps:

  - For each suspect, draw one card representing their personality and one card for the secret they're hiding that makes them appear guilty.

  - Optionally, draw three more cards per suspect, indicating their potential motive, means, and opportunity to commit the crime.

- **Squad Goals**: Think about the people your protagonist spends a lot of story time with. These could be friends, co-workers or colleagues, neighbors, or part of their community in some important way. Draw one card to represent each character's personality. Draw a second card to determine their relationship dynamic with the protagonist. Is this person a friend or foe? Confidante or gossip? Draw a third card to show how this person could positively contribute to your protagonist's aims, and a fourth to represent how they might negatively affect your protagonist's mission.

CHAPTER 5.2

PLOT, SETTING, AND WORLD-BUILDING PROMPTS

PLOT PROMPTS

- **Planting Seeds:** What seeds can you plant early in the story that can grow into something important later on? Draw three cards for inspiration.

- **Security Blanket:** What does your character cling to? What events or circumstances could force them to lose their grip? Draw one card to represent what your character clings to. Draw three to uncover plot events that could push them out of that comfort zone.

- **Coincidence?:** What strange coincidence could your character notice and investigate? Draw one card representing the initial circumstances/details of the coincidence. Draw two more cards to explore deeper layers and potential origins/causes of the coincidence.

- **U-Turn**: Use this spread if you have a specific story direction in mind but are unsure about that direction. What if the opposite happened?

Draw three cards to represent how an alternate to your planned storyline could unfold and impact the rest of the narrative.

- **Leadership**: What story event could force your character to assume a leadership role? How do they react to this development? Draw one card for the event. Draw two to three cards for their reactions.

- **Side Quest!**: What happens to sidetrack your character from pursuing their goal? Draw one to three cards.

- **Reporter's Questions**: Consider what you know about your story so far and identify the missing pieces needed to progress. For those gaps, select some or all of the classic journalistic questions: Who? What? When? Where? Why? and How? Draw one card for each question you want to explore further to develop those missing story elements.

- **Endings and New Beginnings**: What ends for your character in this story? What new beginning does this make space for? Draw two cards--one for endings, one for the new beginning.

- **Emotional Focus**: If you're struggling with a particular scene that feels flat, draw one card to represent its core purpose or emotion. Then, write the scene while keeping the card's meaning and imagery in mind to help bring clarity and focus.

- **Fresh Start**: Who or what would your character like a fresh start with? Draw one to three cards for insight.

- **Problem/Solutions**: What problem does your character encounter in the next scene? What are three possible avenues they can explore to find a solution? Draw one card for the problem and three for potential solutions.

- **Hunch**: What hunch could your character follow to spin the story in a new direction? Draw one card for the hunch. Draw two more cards for the implications of the new direction.

- **Leap of Faith**: What leap of faith could your character take in the story? How does it turn out? Draw one card to represent the leap of faith and two more to determine the outcome.

- **Break**: What could happen that forces your character to slow down and take a break? How does this break help them gain insight into a problem? Draw one card for each question.

- **Plot Twist**: What unexpected development derails your character's plans or makes them reevaluate everything they thought they knew? Draw one to three cards.

- **Motive, Means, and Opportunity**: If your story involves a character attempting to solve a crime, they'll need to evaluate each suspect's motive, means, and opportunity. For each suspect, draw three cards, one to represent motive, one to represent means, and one to represent opportunity.

- **Blast from the Past**: What figure from your character's past could show up unexpectedly and complicate your protagonist's life? Draw one card to represent the person. Draw a second card to represent their relationship to the protagonist. Draw a third card to explore the turmoil that arises from this encounter.

- **Scarcity**: What could your character run out of that forces them to change course or face a person they'd rather avoid? What are the consequences of doing so? Draw one card to determine what they run out of and one to three cards for the consequences.

- **Delay**: What could delay your character in their pursuit? What happens as a result? Draw one card for each question.

- **Inner Obstacle, Outer Obstacle**: If you have an external obstacle planned for your character's next scene, draw a card to add an internal obstacle they must also grapple with. If you already have their inner conflict lined up, draw a card to incorporate a new outer obstacle or complication.

- **Cutting Ties**: Identify who or what your protagonist needs to break away from. Draw one card representing that person/entity. Then draw one card for what they'll lose by cutting ties, and one card for what they'll gain.

- **Double Agent**: Give your character two competing objectives that will generate dramatic tension. Identify two goals for your character. If you don't have both goals in mind, draw one or two cards to represent them. Then, draw three cards to symbolize how these two goals create conflict and tension by pulling your character in different directions.

- **Bias**: What is your character biased about? How does that affect the story's trajectory? Draw one card for each question.

- **Request Denied**: What request could be denied, forcing the protagonist to get creative? Draw one card representing a request or opportunity that gets denied for your protagonist. Then draw three more cards for fresh creative directions your protagonist could pursue after this setback.

- **Subplots**: Need an idea for a subplot to add thematic layers, emotional resonance, or complexity to your narrative? Draw three cards. Think about how the imagery and meanings of each card could inspire a complementary subplot thread that enriches your main story.

- **Fish out of Water**: What situation could make your character feel like an outsider? Draw one to three cards.

- **Plot Holes**: Use this spread when you know some major plot points, but not all of them. Use sticky notes or index cards to map out what you know about the plot. Place blank sticky notes or index cards where there are gaps to fill. Draw a card for each of the holes to help you fill in the gaps.

- **The Tortoise and the Hare**: This is a good spread to use when your character must choose between a short but perilous route and a slower, safer route. Lay out two rows of three cards. The top row represents what might go wrong if they choose the short, perilous route. The bottom row reflects what might go wrong if they choose the slow and steady approach.

- **Under the Surface**: To explore the underlying factors behind your character's next course of action, follow these steps:

    - Draw cards to answer the following questions:

        - What course of action does your character take next? Draw one card.

        - Why do they *say* they want to do it? Draw one card.

        - What additional factors are involved under the surface? Draw one card.

- **Foreshadowing**: What can you add to this scene to foreshadow a later plot event? Draw one to three cards for inspiration.

- **Break the Chain**: What generational traumas or sins of the parent create conflict for your character? How does this impact the story? Draw one card for the source of generational trauma(s). Draw two more for conflicts this creates for your protagonist. Draw two more for story impacts.

- **The Tower**: How can you take a planned conflict and turn it up to an eleven? Draw three cards for insight.

- **Red Herrings**: Use this spread to add misdirection when your character is solving a mystery. Draw three cards for clues that might lead them astray.

- **Breadcrumbs**: Use this spread anytime your character has a mystery to solve. What are the chain of clues your character follows? Draw one card for each clue you need insight about.

- **Wrong Turn**: If you're stuck and can't move forward in your plot, backtrack in your manuscript to see if you can pinpoint a place where you or your characters made a wrong turn that sent things off the rails. Draw one to three cards to inspire an alternative way forward.

- **Breaking Convention**: Think of a rule or norm your character is expected to follow. What would happen if they broke that convention? Draw one card to represent the convention and a second to represent the consequence.

- **GMC Spread:** Draw one card each for your character's goal, motivation, and conflict.

- **MacGuffin**: What important object is everyone in your story after? Why does your character want it? Why does their opponent? What would happen if their opponent got to it first? Draw a card for each question.

- **Beginning, Middle, End:** This is one of the simplest spreads for a big picture story arc. Draw cards to represent the beginning, middle, and end of your story.

- **Three Act Spread**: Use this spread to plan out your major plot events for each section of your story. Draw three cards for events in Act 1. Repeat for Acts 2 and 3.

- **Never Have I Ever:** Play the popular drinking game with your character (or cast of characters). If you're not familiar with the game, it goes like this: One person says something like, "Never have I ever swum with sharks." Participants who *have* done this take a drink. To adapt this as a tarot prompt, imagine you're playing the game with your characters. Draw a card and use something in its imagery or meaning to come up with an "Never Have I Ever" statement. For example, if you drew the Fool, you might notice they are about to walk off a precipice and say, "I've never gone cliff diving." Or if you drew the Three of Swords, you might say, "I've never had my heart broken."

- ○ Variation 1: Imagine how your character would respond. Would they be chugging beer or sticking to a demure sip of their sweet tea?

- ○ Variation 2: Draw a second card for guidance on their response. Odd numbered cards = they have. Evens = they haven't.

- ○ Variation 3: Draw a second card. Use imagery on the card to fill in details and backstory for their answer.

- **Major Story Beat Prompts:** Use these prompts if you're working on a particular beat or section of your story. This is by no means an exhaustive list, but a springboard to get you started. Draw one to three cards to illuminate each aspect you would like to work on.

  - ○ **Ordinary World**: What does your character's ordinary world look like? How do they feel about it?

  - ○ **Memorable Character Introduction**: What circumstances could show off your character's personality as well as their longing and story goal? How does this set of events show each one?

  - ○ **Set-up**: How does your story begin? What's a compelling way to introduce your story world?

- **Inciting Incident/ Catalyst**: What happens to break your character out of their comfort zone and propel them into adventure?

- **Call to Adventure**: What type of call to adventure does your character receive? How do they react? What excuses do they make to resist? Why do they ultimately move forward?

- **Meet Cute**: If you're writing a romance or story with romantic elements, how do the love interests meet or encounter one another for the first time? What are the sparks between them? What are the hesitations of each character about a relationship with the other?

- **The Glue**: What circumstances force the love interests to spend time together? This can also be used with a team or unlikely partners.

- **Meet the Mentor**: Who will serve as a mentor-figure to your character? How do their teachings inspire your character? What creates tension between these characters?

- **Rising Action and Rising Stakes**: What events create increasing tension and obstacles between your character and what they desire? How can you make the stakes higher and more personal for your character?

- **Pinch Points**: What are the moments that put more pressure on your character?

- **Mirror Moment**: What event leads your character to stop and take stock of where they're headed and who they are becoming on their current path? How does this affect what they do next?

- **Set Pieces**: What are some fun audience-pleasing scenes you can add to your story? Some examples might be a chase scene, an explosion, a makeover montage, etc.

- **Major Turning Points**: What events change the course of the story?

- **Midpoint**: What big event, win, setback, or revelation could alter the course of the story at the midpoint?

- **The Point of No Return**: Draw cards to represent the circumstances that force your character to cross a point of no return, where they become fully committed despite potential risks.

- **Temporary Triumph**: What happens to make your protagonist feel like they've won or made progress, even though circumstances will ultimately get complicated and send them back into the fray?

- **Black Moment**: What does it look like for your protagonist when all is lost?

- **Reversal**: How can things turn around in a major way?

- **Obstacles**: Big, Bigger, Biggest. What major obstacles will your characters face in pursuit of their goal?

- **Grand Gesture**: How could a romantic lead pull out all the stops to make a case for a relationship with the other lead?

- **Climax**: What events could happen at the height of the action?

- **Aftermath**: What circumstances result from the climax of your story? How can you show things have changed for the better?

- **Epilogue**: What could a moment of peace, happiness or restored justice look like for your protagonist and cast of characters?

- **Lingering Questions**: If you're writing a series, what questions can you leave in the reader's mind even though you've wrapped up the main plot?

BIG PICTURE PLOT PROMPTS

For those of you who want to see the big picture or an overall story arc, try your hand at more intricate spreads like these.

- **The Fool's Journey Big Picture Plot Spread**: Pull the Major Arcana cards from your deck and lay them out in order. Most decks feature numbered Major Arcana cards. Then shuffle the rest of your deck. Lay one card atop each of the Major Arcana and interpret the meanings based on that point in the journey. For example, if you drew the Four of Wands in the Fool position, your story may starts with your protagonist heading to some kind of celebration or wedding which kicks the story into motion. If you draw the Two of Cups in the Tower position, maybe a close friendship, romantic relationship, or work partnership falls apart, sending the story in a new direction. If you draw the Queen of Pentacles in the Devil position, your character might use busy-ness to bolster their self worth to avoid insecurity.

- **Alternate Big Picture Plot Threads:** Choose your favorite plot structure and look up the beats. Some popular options for fiction writers are Save the Cat, Romancing the Beat, Michael Hauge's Six Stage Plot Structure, The Heroine's Journey, The Hero's Journey and many more. Create index cards or sticky notes representing each beat and lay them out. Draw one card for each beat, interpreting how the card could fit into your story based on the plot beat it represents.

SETTING AND WORLD-BUILDING PROMPTS

- **Setting the Scene to Introduce a New Character:** Draw one to three cards for each of the following:

  - What's the energy of this new character?

- How does your POV character react to this new person?

- What new element does this person bring to the story? (Conflict? Information? More hurdles? Change in power dynamics? A new love interest? A distraction? New responsibilities?)

- What questions is the POV character left with after they encounter this person?

- **Using Setting to Amplify Conflict**: Find a point in your story where tension is high for your character but you're not sold on a particular location. Think about the conflict your character is facing. Draw three cards for inspiration on a setting that could heighten the conflict. For example, if I had a character recovering from addiction and drew the Devil card, that might inspire a scene where the newly-sober protagonist must confront someone who keeps slipping away into bars or a place he used to get high--places he now deliberately avoids--which put him even more off-kilter.

- **Symbolic details**: What imagery or symbols could you include in your settings to hint at larger themes for your book? Draw three cards and examine the symbols on these cards for inspiration.

- **Memorable Setting**: What would make a memorable setting for this story? Draw three cards for inspiration.

- **Home**: What is home like for your character? You can use this as a prompt for their childhood home, or their current home/living space. Draw one to three cards for inspiration.

- **The Price of Magic**: If your story involves magic, what is the cost of using it? Draw three cards.

- **Change of Scenery**: Where could the next scene take place? Draw one card to inspire an unconventional idea.

- **Rite of Passage**: What is a rite of passage in your character's world? How could you include this milestone or ceremony in your story? Draw one card for the rite. Draw two cards for ideas on where it could fit in your story.

CHAPTER 5.3
PROMPTS TO GET YOU UNSTUCK

PROMPTS TO GET YOU UNSTUCK

The prompts in this section are designed to help you move forward from any point in your manuscript. These are especially handy for discovery writers aka "pantsers." You may notice some repetition from the Plotting section. While the prompts in the previous section are meant for looking at the story at a macro-level, similar prompts in this section invite you to consider the questions at the scene level.

- **What's next?** What do I need to know about my character or story events to move forward? Draw one to three cards.

- **Yes or No?** Consider a story question that needs a yes or no answer. Draw one card. Odd numbered cards = yes. Even numbered cards = no. When interpreting this spread, notice how your mind and intuition respond to the yes or no answer. Does it feel off or spot on? Pay more attention to that feeling than the actual outcome of your draw.

- **Inconvenient Emotions:** What inconvenient emotions come up for your character in the next scene? Draw one to three cards for insights.

- **Nostalgia:** What does your character experience in the next scene that elicits nostalgia? What do they feel nostalgic about? Draw one to three cards.

- **Guilty Conscience**: What does your character feel guilty about in the next scene? Draw one to three cards.

- **Awkward**: How can I make this encounter more awkward or fraught for my character? Draw one to three cards.

- **White Lies**: What lie can your character tell in this scene? What's the reason for the lie? Draw two cards, one for the lie and one for the reason.

- **Suspicious**: What does your character suspect someone else is lying about? How does that impact the plot? Draw one card for each question.

- **Something's off Here**: In the next scene, what's not as it seems? Draw one card.

- **Avoidance**: What does your character want to avoid in the next scene? How can you make it almost impossible for them to do so? Draw two to three cards.

- **Misunderstood**: What can your character misunderstand in the next scene? How does that inform their next decision or step? Draw one to three cards.

- **New Point of View:** In the next scene, who or what forces your character to see things from a different perspective? What happens because of this shift? Draw one to three cards.

- **Yes Day**: Imagine your protagonist says yes to something unexpected or out of character in the next scene. What is it? What prompts this decision? Draw one card for each question.

- **That's a No from Me**: Have your character say no to something they'd usually jump at the chance to do. What do they say no to? Why? Draw one card for each question.

- **A Fork in the Road**: Unsure which path to choose? Ask yes or no questions and draw a card for each question. Odd numbers =yes. Even numbers = no.

- **Houdini**: What sleight of hand does your character pull off or witness in the next scene? Draw one to three cards.

- **Bad Vibes**: What bad energy does your character pick up from another in this scene? Draw one card for the source of the bad vibes. Draw one to two more for insights into what's causing this feeling.

- **Hunch**: What hunch could your character follow in this scene? Draw one to three cards to guide you.

- **Leap of Faith**: What leap of faith could your character take in this scene? How does it turn out? Draw one card to represent the leap of faith and two more to determine possible outcomes.

- **Break**: What could happen that forces your character to slow down and take a break in the next scene? How could this break help them gain insight into the problem they're working on? Draw one to three cards.

- **You're on Your Own, Kid**: In the next scene, a person essential to your character's plan doesn't show up. Draw one card to represent the expected person. Draw one card to show how this changes things.

Draw one card to show how your character improvises.

- **Boundaries**: What's an important boundary your character has set for themselves? How can it get pushed or crossed by another character in the next scene? How does your character react? Draw one card for the boundary. Draw one card to illuminate how that boundary could be crossed. Draw one more for your character's reactions.

- **That Niggling Feeling**: What niggling feeling bothers your character in the next scene? Draw one to three cards.

- **Side Quest**: What urgent matter comes up to sidetrack your character from their main goal? Draw one to three cards.

- **Boon**: What unexpected boon does your character receive in the next scene? What negative consequences can it bring along with the positive? Draw one card to represent the boon and two to represent negative consequences.

- **Bad Dream**: What nightmare plagues your character in the next scene? What does it reveal about their worries and preoccupations? Draw one for the nightmare subject. Draw one for revelations about deeper worries.

- **Gathering**: What gathering could your character attend in the next scene? What new piece of insight could be gained from people there? Draw one for the circumstances of the gathering. Draw one to three for the insight uncovered.

- **Ancestral Wisdom**: In the next scene, what wisdom could be passed down from a relative or mentor that changes your protagonist's way of thinking about something? This could come from seeing the person face-to-face, through a story from another relative, or letter, etc. Draw one card to see who the wisdom comes from. Draw one for the message. Draw one for the change in thinking it incites in the protagonist.

- **Wild Card**: Challenge yourself to add a random element to your next scene. Draw a card and add something present on the card to your next scene. This could be something literal, like a concrete object or something inspired by the mood or imagery of the character on the card.

- **It's Complicated**: In the next scene, what could complicate your character's path towards their goal? Draw one to three cards.

- **Cutting Ties**: Who or what does your protagonist need to cut ties with in the next scene? What do they lose if they do? What do they gain? Draw one for the person or organization. Draw one for what they lose. Draw one for what they gain.

- **What's Missing?**: Use this spread when you have a general idea of a plot point, but want to dig deeper. What's missing that could enrich the story? Draw three cards to find out.

- **Stamp of Approval**: Who does your character seek approval from in the next scene? Do they get it? What's their emotional reaction? Draw one card for each of these questions.

- **Open Loops and Don't Close Them Right Away**: What intriguing question or mystery can you plant in the next scene to entice the reader to keep turning pages for the answer? Draw one to three cards for inspiration.

- **Change of Scenery**: What would make a more memorable setting for the next scene? Draw one to three cards for inspiration.

- **And Then What?**: What happens first in the next scene? Draw a card for inspiration. Continue drawing "And Then What?" cards each time you run out of ideas or material.

- **Shower Thoughts**: What's your character thinking about in the shower? Draw one to three cards to find out.

- **Map It Out**: Map out five things that need to happen in the next scene. Draw five cards for insight.

- **Scarcity**: What could your character run out of in the next scene? This could be something tangible like money or a substance needed to perform magic, or more intangible, like patience. What are the consequences? Draw one card to determine what they run out of and one to three cards for the consequences.

- **Disruptor**: What could disrupt your character's carefully laid plan in the next scene (or yours as the author)? Draw one to three cards.

- **Three Things**: Draw three cards to represent three random things to include in the next scene.

- **Yes, and...**: Pull inspiration from the "yes, and..." principle of improv. Draw one card and use it for inspiration for the most unexpected thing that could happen in the next scene. How can you incorporate and build on this to develop the scene?

- **Yes, but...**: Did you give your character what they wanted too soon? If so, what's an unintended consequence that throws another wrench into their plan? Draw one to three cards to find out.

- **No, and or Yes, but**: Unsure of your character's next step? Think about their immediate goal in the next scene. First, draw a card to determine whether they accomplish it. Odd numbered cards = yes. Even numbered cards = no.

  - **No, and...** If your character is thwarted, what's their next step? Draw one card.

  - **Yes, but...** If your character achieves their goal, what additional obstacle or complication comes with the win? Draw one card.

- **Blindfold**: What's your character missing that's right in front of them? Draw one to three cards for inspiration.

- **Subverting Expectations**: What does your character or reader expect to happen next? How can you subvert that expectation? Draw one to three cards to find out.

- **Special Delivery**: What news or mail could your character receive that leads them down an alternative path? Draw one to three cards.

- **Wrong Number**: How can a text, email, etc. from a wrong number provide unexpected insight into solving your character's problem? Draw one to three cards to find out.

- **Loss**: What loss would devastate or kneecap your character right now? How would they protect against it if threatened? Draw two cards, one to represent what the biggest loss would be, and the second to represent how they would protect it if threatened.

- **Opposing Forces**: Who's working against your character right now? How can you make them even more formidable? Draw two cards: one to represent the opposition and the second to provide insight into how you can make them more formidable.

- **Secondary Goal**: What secondary goal in the next scene could add tension or humor? Draw one to three cards to find out.

- **It's Not You, It's Me**: This question is for you, as the author rather than your characters. What's holding me back or keeping me from moving forward? What kind of energy do I need or what question do I need answered to move forward? Draw one to three cards for insight into each of these questions.

- **Character and Crucible**: What kind of challenge can you give your character in the next scene that could present a stepping stone toward reaching their ultimate goal? Draw one to three cards for inspiration.

- **Refresh**: When you're unable to move forward, draw one to three cards for inspiration. Use it as a prompt to write something completely unrelated as a palate cleanser.

Part Six

Interpreting the Cards

CHAPTER 6.1
DIFFERENT WAYS TO INTERPRET THE CARDS

START WITH YOUR IMAGINATION

"We don't see things as they are, we see them as we are."
-Anaïs Nin

Interpretations you assign to the cards depend on the story you want to tell. The same card that represents one story's epic disaster could be another's Hail Mary. Tarot is a mirror: its meanings come from within you, reflecting the ideas, hopes, and fears you channel into your spread.

The tarot opens you up to new ways of thinking about your story, giving you a glimpse of what might happen if you follow a new path. But as the writer, you remain in control of the journey. You choose which crossroads to follow and which to pass by. The tarot can be a sidekick to spark your imagination, but you hold the pen—you decide where the final destination lies.

The interpretation techniques below are there to give you a framework to start with. However, don't be afraid to improvise. Please take what works for you, leave the rest, and tweak and adapt these guidelines to suit your needs.

Interpreting Your Spread

There are many ways to mine your tarot spread for inspiration. You can take a strictly visual approach by examining which imagery and symbols jump out at you, considering the mood of the cards and the associations they bring up.

You can also go a more traditional route and draw on your knowledge of tarot card meanings, use your favorite tarot reference, or the one in this book to look them up. Symbols and numerology corresponding to the cards can add additional layers of meaning.

I like to use a combination of these methods depending on where my subconscious and imagination take me. The way you view the cards in your spreads will depend on your unique perspective, tarot knowledge, and what you already know about your work-in-progress. Sometimes a traditional card meaning or symbol will spark your imagination. Other times, a tiny detail on a card will connect the dots in your story in a way that sets your ideas flowing.

Visual Interpretation

The first method we'll look at for unearthing story clues from the cards is visual interpretation. Similar to a Rorschach inkblot test, the details that stand out and allow us to make sense of what we're seeing draw on our own experiences and viewpoint. Of course, with tarot cards, the symbolism is less abstract.

When you pull a card, spend some time examining the details of it. Look at the images and symbols present. What jumps out at you? What ideas do the visuals trigger related to your story question? Often, just looking at the imagery can pull ideas and memories from your subconscious. You can connect and combine these with what you already had in mind. Other times—these are often the most fun—a tiny detail on the card may set off dominoes of associations that lead you down a delightful path. For example, imagine you pulled The Fool while brainstorming how two characters meet. You notice that the little dog jumping at the Fool's feet looks just like the dog you'd often see at a coffee shop whose bark always sounded like he had a sore throat. Then you remember the last time you saw that dog. You were in an enormous rental car you weren't used to driving. And in your fragile, emotional state preoccupied with big changes and moving company complications, you accidentally backed into the owner's car in the parking lot. Embarrassing memory, but hey, what about a car accident meet cute?

TRADITIONAL MEANING INTERPRETATION

Another tactic is to observe the card and look up the meaning for further insight. You can use the guidebook that came with your deck, a site like T arot.com, or the Storytellers Tarot Reference Guide in Part 7 of this book. I usually cross-reference several guides because each has its own unique spin on a card's significance in the context of their deck's theme. I jot down phrases that resonate and spend some time journaling about how they could apply to my story question. If you're a verbal processor, you may want to talk through your ideas aloud or record your musing for later reference.

COMBINATION

My favorite approach is to combine these two methods to squeeze the greatest amount of input from the cards. I start with visual notes, then move on to the written meanings. They often feed off each other and create additional chains of associations. I encourage you to play with these interpretation techniques and find the approaches that click for you.

REVERSALS

What does it mean if a tarot card is reversed (upside down) when you draw it?

There are several ways to approach reversals when reading tarot for your characters. If you want to keep it simple, just ignore the reversal and interpret the card according to its upright meaning.

Another manner of interpreting reversed tarot cards is to consider the upright meaning and then view the reversal in one of two ways:

1. The reversed card has the opposite meaning of the upright position.

2. The reversed card indicates a blockage or hindrance in the energy typically associated with the upright card.

To better understand this concept, let's examine some examples.

THE DEATH CARD IN REVERSE

The Death card upright is about letting go of the past, shedding old skin, and moving on to the next stage of the path. The reversed meaning might signify trouble moving on or letting go. Or perhaps a character clinging to past patterns that no longer serve.

THE EMPRESS IN REVERSE

Upright, the Empress is all about growth, abundance, fertility, and creativity. Reversed, the Empress might denote stagnation, creative blocks, or infertility.

CHAPTER 6.2
SAMPLE INTERPRETATIONS

To give you an idea of what this looks like in practice, here are some sample interpretations.

SAMPLE ONE: CHARACTER PROMPT

Let's work with this prompt pulled from the character section of the Prompt Library in Part 5:

Prompt

Projection: What trait does your character criticize in others because deep down, it's a trait they dislike in themselves or wish they dared to act on? Draw one card.

Imagine we drew the Eight of Cups. Take a few minutes and notice what jumps out at you on the card image. Think about how it could apply to the character prompt.

Eight of Cups

VISUAL INTERPRETATION

Here are some elements you might notice on the Eight of Cups card:

- A lone figure with a walking stick trekking away from eight full cups

- A rocky, uphill path ahead

- Eight golden cups left behind

- A full moon donning a somber expression

- Mountains and greenery in the distance

- Clear blue sky

- Still waters

- Loose red tunic, pants, and boots

Now, let's look at how we could interpret each detail in terms of the trait your character criticizes in others because deep down, it's something they dislike about themselves or wish they had the courage to act on:

A lone figure with a walking stick trekking away from eight full cups

- Refusal of generosity and offers of help

- The ability to walk away from a situation that no longer serves them, despite it being the harder path.

- The ability to walk away from old patterns

- The ability to resist the temptations of stability and resources and leave with nothing but the clothes on their back

- Impulsively leaving situations when they seem too good to be true

- Freedom to travel

- Failure to plan for trips (My dude doesn't even have a pack. Even the Fool, the greenest card in the deck, had the forethought to pack a small bag.)

- The luxury of leaving the emotional labor of planning and packing to someone else

A rocky, uphill path ahead

- Stubbornly taking the hard way when more experienced people have advised against it.

- Doing something hard to prove a point

- Fighting uphill battles

Eight golden cups left behind

- Carelessness with resources

- Wealth and privilege

- Waste, excess

- Embarking on a fool's errand to find a mythical object like the Holy Grail

- Drinking and then walking away from the problems they create while intoxicated

A full moon donning a somber expression

- A somber outlook

- Reliance on intuition instead of logic

- Not being able to see something right in front of their nose even with a spotlight shining on it

- Keeping secrets, keeping parts of themselves unknowable

Mountains and greenery in the distance

- Growth that your character can't or won't seek for themselves

- Choosing a path toward stability instead of spontaneity

Clear blue sky

- A naively optimistic outlook

- An unworried attitude

Still waters

- Taking the easy way

- Being too emotional

- Crying

- Indulging in self-reflection

- The ability to talk about their feelings

- An uncomplicated life, when their own is rife with turmoil

Loose red tunic, pants, and boots

- Hippie fashion choices

- Choosing comfort over fashion

- Comfort in disregard for traditional clothing

- The freedom to wear clothes made for movement rather than skirts corsets and petticoats

TRADITIONAL MEANINGS INTERPRETATION FOR THE EIGHT OF CUPS

- Recognizing when it's time to walk away

- Retreating instead of continuing to fight

- Emotional detachment

- Letting go

- Recognizing sunk costs

- Strategic quitting

- Abandonment and escapism

SAMPLE TWO: PLOT PROMPT

Let's work with this prompt pulled from the Plot/Setting section of the Prompt Library in Part 5:

Prompt

Plot Twist: What happens to throw a wrench into your character's plans? Draw one to three cards for inspiration.

Imagine we drew the Empress Card. Take a few minutes and notice what jumps out at you on the card image. Think about how it could apply to this plot prompt.

The Empress

VISUAL INTERPRETATION

Here are some elements you might notice on the Empress card:

- A woman seated on a throne-like chair with cushy pillows

- A crown of stars

- Plentiful wheat and greenery

- Water

- A dress with pomegranates on it

- The woman appears pregnant (not in the Rider Waite Smith deck, but in many others).

Now, let's look at how we could interpret each detail in terms of a plot twist.

A woman seated on a throne-like chair with cushy pillows

- An injury leads to unexpected bed rest.

- Your character is distracted or dazzled by offered comforts.

- Your character learns they are part of a royal bloodline.

- Someone unexpected offers comfort.

The woman appears pregnant.

- Secret baby trope

- Your character finds or takes a pregnancy test.

- Someone tells your character they're pregnant.

A crown of stars

- Your character discovers they are celestial royalty.

- Your character meets an astronaut.

- Your character is invited to a fancy star-themed ball.

Plentiful wheat and greenery

- Your character usually kills every plant they try to keep, but suddenly all of their plants proliferate and take over their apartment.

- Something strange happens at a harvest festival.

- Your character inherits a brewery.

Water

- The place where your character is trapped is filling with water.

- At a magic show, someone tampers with the water tank used in an illusion, and the magician drowns.

- Mysterious watery footsteps materialize in your character's home.

A dress with pomegranates on it

- Hades and Persephone-inspired twist?

- Your character receives a box of pomegranates with an ominous note.

- Just before an important meeting, someone spills pomegranate juice all over your protagonist's dress.

TRADITIONAL MEANINGS INTERPRETATION FOR THE EMPRESS

Your plot twist could be...

- The sudden appearance of a mother figure your protagonist believed to be dead

- A genetic mutation

- Your protagonist can control flowers and plants.

- Mother Nature sends a terrible storm.

- An alien plant sprouts and causes chaos.

- Discovery of corruption at the botanical garden

SAMPLE THREE: GET UNSTUCK PROMPT

Let's work with this prompt pulled from the Prompts to Get You Unstuck section of the Prompt Library in Part 5:

Prompt

Blindfold: What's your character missing that's right in front
of them? Draw one to three cards for inspiration. This one is
great for mysteries.

Imagine we drew the Star Card. Take a few minutes and notice what jumps out at you on the card image. Think about how it could apply to the prompt.

The Star

VISUAL INTERPRETATION

Here are some elements you might notice on the Star card:

- A naked woman pouring two jugs of water, one into a pond and the other onto the shore

- A bird

- A constellation of stars overhead, though it looks like daytime

Now, let's look at how we could interpret each detail in terms of a blind spot.

A naked woman is pouring two jugs of water, one into a pond and the other onto the shore.

- Sleight of hand: What if, when they saw the suspect pour out one drink, they missed what that person was doing with the other hand?

- A person who appears to be an open book is hiding something.

- Nudity or other shock techniques could have been used as misdirection.

- A corporation is secretly dumping chemicals into the groundwater.

- A person is feeding info to both competitors.

- A suspect is secretly living in a local park and washing up in the lake.

A bird

- A parrot could have overheard a fight and repeated key information.

- A bird nest camera installed on the victim's property could hold evidence everyone has overlooked.

- A gossipy neighbor has details ("A little birdie told me...").

A constellation of stars appears overhead, though it looks like daytime.

- The suspect's timeline doesn't match up.

- The drawing they saw earlier was a star map.

- Discovery of a secret coded message that can only be seen during the daytime.

- A suspect's celebrity connections have shielded them from the repercussions of their actions.

TRADITIONAL MEANINGS INTERPRETATION FOR THE STAR CARD

Your character's blind spot could be...

- Ignoring intuition

- The visionary did it

- A healer or otherwise "good" person can also be capable of harmful actions.

- Someone's squeaky clean image masks dark secrets.

With some cards, you'll find a good deal of crossover between your visual interpretation and what you find as you analyze the traditional meanings. I encourage you to try both ways to discover what resonates most with you. Combine the info you get from each method to amplify or complement one another. Feel free to mix and match in a way that feels most helpful for each prompt.

Sample Tarot Journal Entry

Writing down your ideas and impressions and free-associating can also trigger even deeper insights. Here's a sample of the tarot journal format I use to record my spread notes:

Project:

Question/ What I need help with:

Prompt:

Deck:

Card(s):

Observations:

Meaning Notes:

Connections to Story Question/Other Thoughts:

Part Seven

The Storyteller's Tarot Reference Guide

CHAPTER 7.1

UNDERSTANDING THE MAJOR ARCANA

The Major Arcana consists of the first twenty-two cards in the tarot, from (0) The Fool to (21) The World. As we discussed in the introduction to the tarot section, these cards lay the foundation for a story. The Fool, the avatar for your protagonist, sets off on a new adventure, meets allies and enemies, faces challenges and setbacks, and gains the hard-earned wisdom necessary for the culmination of their story. If your book has a happy ending, The World is where your main character(s) find purpose and meaning from the events they've weathered along the way.

Traditionally, **the Major Arcana** represent **big-picture life events**. I like to think of them as milestone cards. Each one represents a pivotal moment or encounter that shapes your character's journey and story as it unfolds.

There are two main ways to incorporate the Major Arcana into your writing process. First, you can use the Fool's Journey and the Major Arcana as a whole to create a story framework. If you like to plan stories and develop your major beats in advance, Major Arcana cards are great for helping expand on the important events and figures in your narrative.

Second, you can use Major Arcana cards individually as part of any chosen prompt. For those of you who prefer discovering the story as you go, these cards can liven up your chapters or derail your characters along the way. If you know you need a significant moment, separate the Major Arcana from the rest of the deck and draw from them.

In the rest of this section, you'll explore the meanings of each of the twenty-two Major Arcana cards. This Tarot for Storytellers Guide includes not only the basics, but also more detailed insights for writers, offering suggestions on how each card could be interpreted in terms of character, plot, Potential Story Conflict, or relationship conflict.

0 - THE FOOL

Basic Meaning: Represents new beginnings, innocence, and spontaneity.

Character: Depicts an individual at the beginning of their journey, characterized by naïveté and optimism.

Traits and archetypes the Fool card could reflect: The Fool card could reflect any character at the precipice of a journey into uncharted territory. They could be a young, idealistic character, innocent and full of wonder. However, taking a leap of faith is hardly reserved for the young. The Fool could also signify characters taking a chance on a new career, discovering magical powers at midlife, or starting over after a breakup or loss. Fool characters could also manifest as someone taking chances, such as cliff jumping, skydiving, or engaging in adventure sports, embracing the thrill of the unknown.

Potential Positive Traits: This character is eager and brave, ready to step out of their comfort zone with an up-for-anything attitude. They sometimes exude a childlike wonder. They have the courage to be vulnerable and often wear their heart on their sleeve.

Potential Shadow Traits: On the flip side, they can be impulsive and naïve, often ill-prepared. Their readiness to dive in head-first with their "ready-fire-aim" tendencies may lead to trouble. They can be childish, immature, or give up before they begin.

Themes: Learning from mistakes, blind spots/not knowing what you don't know, optimism pays off, leap of faith.

Plot: In the story, a journey begins, a new opportunity emerges, the protagonist develops a new power or gets called away on an unexpected assignment.

Potential Story Conflict: Throughout the plot, conflict arises from recklessness and bad decisions, as well as lack of preparation.

Potential Relationship Conflict: In relationships, friction may result from flightiness and the tendency to act impulsively. Risky investments and naïve decisions create tension.

1 - THE MAGICIAN

Basic Meaning: Represents potential, the ability to take action, and manifesting desires.

Character: Depicts a character who possesses or can gather all the skills and tools necessary to manifest goals. This person is creative and resourceful.

Traits and archetypes the Magician card could reflect: This character is a catalyst, an instigator, and creator with untapped potential. They might be a charismatic charmer, a powerful sorceress or mage, or a chosen one, and may have a selfish streak. This character might work in a creative field, such as architecture, choreography, painting, sculpture, writing, digital art, or engineering.

Potential Positive Traits: This character possesses ingenuity, inventiveness, and resourcefulness, along with power over mental and psychic abilities. They excel at conveying ideas effectively and are adaptable and witty.

Potential Shadow Traits: This character could also be manipulative, using illusions for selfish or nefarious purposes, and often tempted to deceive others. They may take wonder for granted, and have an inflated sense of power, craving control, showing off, or stirring up drama.

Themes: Themes revolve around coming into one's own power, living up to potential, or making dreams a reality by manifesting desires.

Plot: In the plot, the character takes action and harnesses their talents to solve problems.

Potential Story Conflict: Deception or using skills unethically creates turmoil.

Potential Relationship Conflict: In relationships, conflicts may arise from manipulation, unclear communication, gaslighting, the use of smoke and mirrors, or the realization that things are not as they seem.

2 - THE HIGH PRIESTESS

Basic Meaning: Represents intuition, sacred knowledge, and the divine feminine.

Character: This individual is intuitive, deeply connected to inner wisdom, a spiritual leader, and often secretive.

Traits and archetypes the High Priestess card could reflect: This character may be a mystic, sage, or an oracle, perhaps someone with psychic or psychometric powers. They could also be a reincarnated priestess, a practitioner of yoga, a tarot reader, or enthusiast of mindfulness and meditation. Often mysterious and enigmatic, they serve as soulful guides and keepers of secrets.

Potential Positive Traits: High Priestess-inspired characters are intuitive and possess wisdom beyond their years, with a calm and centered presence. They're excellent listeners and offer insightful guidance and nurturing to those seeking it. They're protective of sacred or private matters, such as family or personal issues, and seek self-knowledge through reflection.

Potential Shadow Traits: The character could also be distant, aloof, and overly secretive, often withholding information. They may gloat about knowing secret details that seem inaccessible to others.

Themes: Themes revolve around uncovering mysteries, learning to listen to your intuition, or the repercussions of disclosing or unearthing secrets. Think opening Pandora's box, Eve tasting the forbidden fruit, or Blackbeard's bride unlocking the one forbidden room.

Plot: In the plot, the character struggles to trust their inner voice and grapples with the repercussions of disclosing secrets. They also face danger from individuals seeking their secret knowledge.

Potential Story Conflict: Potential conflicts include dealing with mystery, uncertainty, or hidden agendas. Access to esoteric knowledge, sacred items, or hidden objects could also create conflict. Characters may deal with fears regarding their unique powers or abilities.

Potential Relationship Conflict: In relationships, conflicts arise from secrets, perhaps the inability to share classified information, leading to tension and mistrust between partners.

3 - THE EMPRESS

Basic Meaning: Symbolizes creativity, growth, fertility, abundance, nature, femininity, and beauty.

Character: This character is nurturing, supportive, abundant, and sensual.

Traits and archetypes the Empress card could reflect: The character could take the role of a mother, artist, nurturer, or caregiver, embodying traits of fertility and nurturing. They may be drawn to jobs that involve the natural world or creation in some capacity. Empresses may be gardeners, conservationists, or genetic scientists. They thrive in nature and possess a powerful drive to create in their chosen area of artistic expression. Empresses may also feel a need to reinvent themselves.

Potential Positive Traits: This character is warm and welcoming, a good listener, and empathetic. They possess strong maternal instincts and grace under pressure, with a generous spirit and an encouragement of others' gifts. If they want no children of their own, they may be the mama bear of their friend group. They're prolific creators and have a sensual nature, feeling connected to all things and exuding lush qualities.

Potential Shadow Traits: The character tends to be overprotective, displaying traits of a helicopter parent or tiger mother, and can become smothering or indulgent, sometimes leading to laziness or complacency.

Themes: Themes include the ability to create what you desire and discovering abundance where scarcity was perceived, as well as the rewards of nurturing others.

Plot: In the plot, creativity blossoms, new life springs forth, potentially unsettling others and disrupting the status quo.

Potential Story Conflict: Potential conflicts involve overindulgence, feeling overwhelmed as things grow too quickly, and neglecting personal needs while focusing on nurturing others.

Potential Relationship Conflict: In relationships, conflicts may arise from possessiveness, jealousy, and over protectiveness regarding one's creations.

4 - THE EMPEROR

Basic Meaning: Represents authority, structure, and control.

Character: Depicts an authority figure or leader. This could be someone who's structured or controlling.

Traits and archetypes the Emperor could reflect: The character exudes the qualities of a ruler or warrior: authoritative, strong-willed, and structured. They're logical, disciplined, and protective, often seen as a father-figure. Emperors may be found in various roles, such as corporate executive, thought leader, politician, movie producer/director, or orchestra conductor. They are stoic and self-possessed, adept at setting and maintaining boundaries.

Potential Positive Traits: The character is a protector of their family or community, known for making fair and just decisions. They're reliable, steadfast, and remain calm under pressure, exemplifying responsible leadership. Their actions provide stability and structure, and they are known for being action-oriented.

Potential Shadow Traits: The character can also be rigid, inflexible, and display a distant, aloof demeanor. They prioritize strategy over empathy, sometimes leading to outbursts and micro-management. They can be authoritarian, dictatorial, stubborn, and prone to being selfish and self-aggrandizing, often being bullheaded or forceful.

Themes: Themes include structure and order, emphasizing sound leadership and authority.

Plot: In the plot, the character focuses on building order and systems, consolidating power.

Potential Story Conflict: Potential conflicts involve tyranny, inflexibility, and the abuse of power.

Potential Relationship Conflict: In relationships, conflicts may arise from dominance, stubbornness, corruption, or the struggle for control.

5 - THE HIEROPHANT

Basic Meaning: Represents tradition, conformity, and morality.

Character: Depicts a character who is traditional, conventional, and a staunch upholder of belief systems.

Traits and archetypes the Hierophant card could reflect: The character exhibits traits of a teacher and guide, known for being ritualistic, conforming, and traditional. Structured and learned, they may be religious leaders, gurus, or cult leaders. They may be masters in their field, guiding others as a mentor or leading a movement with charisma. However, they might also be at home running an MLM or Ponzi scheme, or adopting a monk-like lifestyle.

Potential Positive Traits:: The character brings stability through teaching, upholding moral standards, and preserving a group's sacred traditions. They promote community and unity, respecting customs and serving as a wise counselor. They nurture spiritual growth and hunger for knowledge.

Potential Shadow Traits: The character could also be dogmatic and inflexible, displaying power-hungry behavior and using their status to exploit others. They may be hypocritical, clinging to the past or outdated ways, and judgmental, adopting a holier-than-thou attitude. They may feel above the law and exhibit self-righteousness.

Themes: Themes include considering the relevance of traditions and beliefs, the tension between conformity and freethinking, and the struggle to break free from structural repression. They could also center on the disconnection from the community due to non-conformist beliefs, or highlighting the potential for growth with support.

Plot: The plot might revolve around adherence to established rules and structures, significant rites of passage, and the battle against the establishment, showcasing the clash between old and new ways.

Potential Story Conflict: Potential story conflicts arise from strict orthodoxy, the refusal to challenge the status quo, mob mentality, the isolation experienced in positions of power, misplaced faith, and loss of community due to unconventional thoughts or behaviors.

Potential Relationship Conflict: In relationships, the story could explore the consequences of rigidity and closed-mindedness, where hypocritical actions and the exploitation of status and power lead to dominance over others and ensuing conflict.

6 - THE LOVERS

Basic Meaning: Represents love, choice, and duality.

Character: Depicts a character having to make a choice, someone torn between options, or intimate bonds and connections between characters.

Traits and archetypes the Lovers card could reflect: The character could take on the essence of the lover, the partner, soul mate, or the epitome of romantic ideals. They may or may not live up to that idealistic vision. They thrive in intimate relationships, acting as a companion, deeply connected, trusting, and cherishing their partner. Marked by passion, they are the romantic idealist, perhaps a poet or a hopeless romantic, seeking an equal partner or twin flame.

Potential Positive Traits: The character is a great communicator, emotionally available, and adept at balancing intimacy with independence or interdependence, showing devotion as a partner. They value honesty and strive for understanding and compromise, ensuring mutual care and respect in their romantic relationships.

Potential Shadow Traits: Character traits can also include jealousy, possessiveness, and clinginess, often leading to smothering and co-dependent behaviors with poor boundaries and dependency issues. They struggle with compromising in relationships.

Themes: Themes revolve around making important choices, understanding relationship values, and navigating the balance between attraction and connection. Relationships require both attraction and effort to maintain a healthy balance between intimacy and personal space.

Plot: In the plot, characters face an important decision amid an imbalance in their relationship, highlighting unhealthy dependency.

Potential Story Conflict: Potential conflicts involve indecision, internal tension between head and heart, and the risk of losing one's identity by giving away too much power.

Potential Relationship Conflict: In relationships, conflicts may manifest as love triangles, conflicting desires, and struggles with independence and dependency. Fear of intimacy, trust issues, and insecurities may lead to self-sabotage.

7 - THE CHARIOT

Basic Meaning: Represents direction, control, and willpower.

Character: Depicts a character who is confident, self-disciplined, and victorious over obstacles.

Traits and archetypes the Chariot card could reflect: The character embodies the spirit of adventure, championing causes and conquering challenges with strategic prowess. They know how to make a grand entrance and are adept at uniting opposing forces. Whether as a commanding officer or in personal pursuits, they approach every endeavor with a single-minded determination and meticulously planned strategies, always driven by a desire to prove themselves.

Potential Positive Traits: The character possesses a strong work ethic and exercises mastery over their impulses and emotions. They are strategic and tactical thinkers, approaching challenges with a calm and composed demeanor. Confidently facing obstacles, they remain goal-focused throughout.

Potential Shadow Traits: This character is also prone to tunnel vision and can be strident, forceful, and intimidating, driven by an intense, competitive nature. They struggle to adapt to changes and are relentless, restless, and impatient in their pursuits, often disregarding others' needs.

Themes: Themes center on willpower, self-control, overcoming obstacles, persistence, or a union of opposites.

Plot: In the plot, the character charges ahead relentlessly to achieve victory or restore honor, driven by a desire to prove themselves.

Potential Story Conflict: Potential conflicts include inflexibility and the risk of burnout as the Chariot's relentless drive pushes themselves and others beyond healthy limits.

Potential Relationship Conflict: In relationships, conflicts arise from competitiveness, arguments over direction, and intolerance of those who don't match the Chariot's obsessive drive. Their forceful and intimidating manner may alienate others, and their laser focus on goals can lead to neglect of interpersonal relationships in favor of success.

8 - STRENGTH

Basic Meaning: Represents inner power, courage, and compassion.

Character: Depicts a character who's patient and compassionate, with quiet inner strength.

Traits and archetypes the Strength card could reflect: The character embraces the roles of the hero, protector, guardian, warrior, peacemaker, and sage, serving as a protective friend or lover and having a deep affinity for animals.

Potential Positive Traits: The character possesses the remarkable ability to remain soft despite adversity. They are deeply empathetic and exhibit fortitude and emotional resilience. In-tune with nature, they possess a tenacious spirit and inner calm, able to stand up for others while balancing brute strength with vulnerability.

Potential Shadow Traits: The character can be prone to caregiver fatigue or struggle with repressing their own emotions, making it difficult for them to assert their own needs. They have a tendency to enable others' flaws or bad choices in the name of being supportive and can be overly compliant and people-pleasing.

Themes: Themes revolve around inner strength, courage in facing adversity or dangerous situations, and viewing vulnerability as a source of strength. Strength-inspired characters seek healing and aim to bring harmony to opposing forces, reconciling conflicting aspects of their identity while learning to trust.

Plot: In the plot, characters grapple with taming wild urges or bringing harmony to chaos. They sometimes take on more than they can handle and fail to address their own needs.

Potential Story Conflict: Potential conflicts include repressed emotions boiling over, passive aggression, finding the balance between courage and compassion, managing primal instincts, and confronting the darker aspects of their psyche.

Potential Relationship Conflict: In relationships, conflicts may come from withholding affection as punishment, resenting time spent caring for others, being overly yielding, giving up too much of oneself, and engaging in power struggles.

9 - THE HERMIT

Basic Meaning: Represents contemplation, search for truth, and inner guidance.

Character: Depicts a character who's a wise mentor or someone retreating into isolation to do some soul-searching.

Traits and archetypes the Hermit card could reflect: The character embodies roles such as the sage, hermit, scholar, seeker, monk, elder, and introspective individual, known for their wisdom and solitude.

Potential Positive Traits: This character is self-aware and reflective, comfortable with their own thoughts and company. They rely on their experiences to navigate life and find contentment in being alone, drawing upon their inner resources and resilience.

Potential Shadow Traits: The character may be socially withdrawn and struggle to connect with others, often finding it hard to break free from their own thoughts. They may have escapist tendencies and be judgmental of the outside world, withholding connection and lacking in people skills. They're often seen as loners or shut-ins, overly independent and withdrawn.

Themes: Themes center around the importance of looking within oneself, even when it's uncomfortable, finding wisdom through seclusion and soul-searching, and feeling out of sync with the world.

Plot: In the plot, the character retreats from society for reflection, experiencing illumination through solitude before eventually returning to society, though this can lead to conflicts and challenges.

Potential Story Conflict: Potential story conflicts include feelings of alienation, reluctance to re-engage with the world, and difficulties adjusting after a period of detachment, all while balancing thoughts and actions.

Potential Relationship Conflict: In relationships, conflicts may stem from emotional distance and shutdown, as well as anxiety about being alone. Hermits may also struggle with judgment towards those who don't prioritize quiet contemplation.

10 - THE WHEEL OF FORTUNE

Basic Meaning: Represents change, cycles, fate, and karma.

Character: Depicts a character who is subject to cycles of change, fate, and the randomness of life's twists and turns.

Traits and archetypes the Wheel of Fortune card could reflect: This character is associated with fate, destiny, and lady luck, embodying traits of a gambler, a flexible traveler, and a survivor. They're often seen as eternal students, with a mercurial or capricious nature.

Potential Positive Traits: The character is adaptable to change and learns from life's ups and downs, displaying a resilient spirit and an ability to roll with the punches. They're optimistic, seizing opportunities and living in the moment, often considered fortunate.

Potential Shadow Traits: The character could also feel unfortunate or cheated by fate, adopting a fatalistic or nihilistic outlook. They often complain about bad luck, blaming external factors and resenting losses while taking wins for granted. They may also feel anxious about uncertainty.

Themes: Themes include karma and navigating experiences beyond our control, as well as learning to let go of control and finding meaning in misfortune.

Plot: The plot may involve sudden reversals or turns of events beyond one's control. It might be serendipity bringing two people together or chaos disrupting someone who thrives on order. A lucky break may also send the story in a new direction.

Potential Story Conflict: Potential story conflicts include dealing with bad luck or a change of luck, facing the consequences of karma, or navigating changes caused by serendipitous events.

Potential Relationship Conflict: In relationships, conflicts may have roots in blaming others for unwanted changes, resenting a partner for unexpected circumstances, adopting a victim mentality, avoiding responsibility, or denying the role of chance in situations. Friction can result when one person clings to an imagined perfect outcome.

11 - JUSTICE

Basic Meaning: Represents fairness, truth, and law.

Character: Depicts a character who exemplifies ethical principles, fairness, and a commitment to upholding truth, displaying a discerning and fair-minded nature.

Traits and archetypes the Justice card could reflect: The character could be a judge, lawmaker, arbiter, or upholder of the law, embodying qualities of an executioner or referee. They are impartial and law-abiding, serving as fair and just judges.

Potential Positive Traits: This character is a truth-seeker, just, and balanced, known for their principled and fair-minded approach. They remain objective and uphold rules equitably, always seeking ethical resolutions and championing fairness. They are idealistic and have integrity, consistently taking responsibility and doing what's right, even in challenging circumstances.

Potential Shadow Traits: The character is often seen as rigid and by-the-book, detached and unemotional in their approach. They can be punitive rather than restorative and may display hypocrisy in their judgments, sometimes abusing their power or status.

Themes: Themes focus on accountability, cause and effect, or the mismatch between ethics and legality. Mercy and the recognition that life isn't always fair can also be themes associated with the Justice card, as well as the weight of responsibility for difficult choices.

Plot: In the plot, characters may face consequences for their actions, grapple with abuse of authority, or the scales may be tipped against someone.

Potential Story Conflict: Potential story conflicts include harsh over-correction, selective application of rules, or bias in the justice system. Problems can also stem from putting what is lawful above what is just, idealism vs. reality, a choice between two evils, or facing a hard truth.

Potential Relationship Conflict: In relationships, conflicts may bubble up from assigning blame instead of finding compromise, inflexibility, or prioritizing truth-telling at the expense of others' feelings. Impartiality may cause rifts, especially when one person is jaded while the other remains idealistic, or when one resorts to shaming others to bolster their own sense of righteousness.

12 – The Hanged One/The Hanged Man

Basic Meaning: Represents new perspective, sacrifice, waiting, and purposeful introspection.

Character: Depicts a character seeing from a new perspective, a martyr, or someone sacrificing for a higher cause.

Traits and archetypes the Hanged One card could reflect: The character embodies the essence of a mystic, martyr, observer, shaman, or iconoclast, displaying qualities of being suspended, surrendered, patient, receptive, and unconventional.

Potential Positive Traits: This character exhibits openness to new experiences and a willingness to learn and adapt. They maintain inner stillness even in times of turmoil and can easily adopt new perspectives. Empathetic and open-minded, they are reflective and flexible thinkers, comfortable embracing uncertainty. Their introspection serves a purpose, guiding their growth and understanding.

Potential Shadow Traits: The character may wrestle with indecision, often getting stuck in analysis paralysis and feeling overwhelmed by options. They may avoid commitments, be easily influenced or ignore their instincts. When lacking problem-solving skills, they lead an unexamined life and exhibit close-mindedness and stubbornness.

Themes: Themes revolve around letting go of ego and considering new perspectives, requiring sacrifice and surrendering certainty to explore new angles of a problem. Gaining new insight often demands surrender.

Plot: In the plot, the character experiences a transformative journey of letting go, encountering reversals, or pausing to gain new perspectives. The plot could also involve surrender of a previous worldview in light of new information.

Potential Story Conflict: Potential story conflicts include being stuck in limbo or reluctance to move forward, as well as the struggle of a passive character being thrust into an active role. There may be resistance to surrender and a tendency to hold on to things that no longer serve them.

Potential Relationship Conflict: In relationships, conflicts may come from the unwillingness to change or adapt. One person's willingness to let go of preconceptions and gain new perspectives can create discord with another who clings to old ways of thinking. Suspending shared habits to gain new insights may also make one person uncomfortable.

13 - DEATH

Basic Meaning: Represents endings, new beginnings, change, and transformation.

Character: Depicts a character who must accept impermanence, undergo transformation, or release the past.

Traits and archetypes the Death card could reflect: The character embodies transition, change, and the shedding of old skin, akin to the reaper, butterfly, or phoenix. They may be a recent divorcée starting over, a character undergoing a makeover montage, or entering the witness protection program to start fresh.

Potential Positive Traits: The character releases attachments and welcomes new phases of life, showing adaptability to change and evolution. They make room for renewal and accept impermanence, viewing endings as a natural part of life.

Potential Shadow Traits: The character is resistant to change and tends to brood over losses, often missing warning signs of decay. They may appear cold and cling to dead dreams, driven by fear or denial of mortality. This can lead to destructive behavior, even courting death because of shame or guilt.

Themes: Themes include beginnings and endings, the cycles of life, dealing with the death of a loved one, grief, starting over, rebirth, reinvention, metamorphosis, and exits.

Plot: In the plot, the story revolves around the end of a cycle, significant changes, and the old giving way to the new. Characters may struggle with fighting change, embark on a quest for immortality, or try to cheat death. In some cases, a character may return as a ghost.

Potential Story Conflict: Potential conflicts include resistance to change, fear of the unknown, holding onto outdated dreams, and grief or sentimental attachments hindering character progression.

Potential Relationship Conflict: In relationships, conflicts may ensue from holding onto what must evolve, remaining in a relationship that no longer serves either party, or allowing the past to intrude on the present. Ignoring warning signs of trouble can also lead to conflicts.

14 - TEMPERANCE

Basic Meaning: Represents balance, moderation, harmony, synthesis, and synergy.

Character: Depicts a character who is balancing opposites, achieving harmony, or moderation.

Traits and archetypes the Temperance card could reflect: This character serves as a mediator, harmonizer, diplomat, sage, counselor, and go-between. They evoke the concept of yin and yang, acting as an arbitrator, hostage negotiator, or alchemist.

Potential Positive Traits: This character favors cooperation over conflict, carefully measuring their actions. They exude a peacemaking presence, remaining calm, patient, and composed. Intuitive and adept at synthesizing extremes, they show prudence and moderation. Comfortable with paradoxes, they excel at managing disparate personalities.

Potential Shadow Traits: The character may sometimes be too cautious or indecisive, attempting to appease both sides and enabling extremism. They might lack assertiveness, dampening valid differences, and repressing emotions because of people-pleasing tendencies.

Themes: Themes include balance, moderation, and learning to live in the middle instead of at extremes, emphasizing the importance of finding middle ground and recognizing nuance.

Plot: In the plot, the story revolves around blending and synthesizing, reaching middle ground, perhaps within a newly blended family or group.

Potential Story Conflict: Potential story conflicts may emerge from extremes of behavior, unwillingness to compromise, and clashes of interests. Dealing with polarities and running from conflict may create further problems.

Potential Relationship Conflict: In relationships, conflicts may pop up from power struggles and a need for better emotional balance. Lack of firmness can lead to resentment when boundaries are inevitably crossed, and differing communication styles may also cause tension, such as cooperation versus conflict-based approaches.

15 - THE DEVIL

Basic Meaning: Represents the shadow self, addiction, attachments, and materialism.

Character: A character associated with this card is often hedonistic, bound to addictions or attachments, or ruled by primal desires.

Traits and archetypes the Devil card could reflect: The character could be a shadow-dweller, someone struggling with vices, or a prisoner of instinct. They may be self-indulgent, driven by or mentally enslaved to their carnal or earthly desires. They could also be an unreliable narrator.

Potential Positive Traits: Potential positive traits of this character include willingness to confront their shadow side for insights, seeking balance in indulgences, and focusing on personal growth and evolution. They strive for freedom, work to break unhealthy bonds, and demonstrate self-awareness by acknowledging their darker sides. They appreciate the lessons learned from facing their shadow and look for healthy ways to unleash it.

Potential Shadow Traits: This character may make excuses for toxic habits or avoid facing unpleasant truths by self-medicating and using fun to evade responsibility. They may create dependence in others, manipulate, take advantage of others, and exhibit vanity. There's also a tendency toward schadenfreude, feeling helpless to break ties with vices, and constructing false narratives to justify actions.

Themes: Themes may explore compulsion, addiction, and being bound by earthly desires. Alongside these, characters may reconcile numbing their feelings with work, or substances, and the struggle to break unhealthy bonds while seeking balance between base desires and higher aims.

Plot: In the plot, temptation may be a central driver, with the character's shadow side in control, leading to mental or physical enslavement and self-limiting behaviors.

Potential Story Conflict: Potential story conflicts could arise from destructive obsessions, hard lessons through excess, repression of the dark side leading to an explosion of darkness, and the character lying to oneself or others. They may also be consumed by the promise of pleasure, status, power, or money, perhaps even selling their soul for the promise of the thing they crave.

Potential Relationship Conflict: In relationships, conflicts may include enabling, codependency, abuse, and manipulation. For instance, one character may avoid reality while the other struggles with rehab or AA, or there may be an inability to delay gratification.

16 - THE TOWER

Basic Meaning: Signifies sudden change, chaos, revelation, and breaking down to build back up.

Character: This character is often disruptive, serving as a catalyst of change and shattering worldviews. They may be seen as revolutionary or radical.

Traits and archetypes the Tower card could reflect: This character may be an earth shaker, revolutionary, phoenix, survivor, alchemist, instigator, or button-pusher.

Potential Positive Traits: This character adapts quickly to crisis, builds new foundations, and sees potential in the ruins. They look for lessons and helpers in the upheaval, and emerge stronger and more resilient from the experience. They are opportunistic in breakdowns, taking hard lessons to heart.

Potential Shadow Traits: This character may ignore signs of looming disaster, attributing blame to outside forces and failing to course-correct. They might act rashly out of panic and resist the necessary destruction and dismantling of outdated systems, remaining stuck in devastation and adopting unhealthy coping mechanisms after a crisis.

Themes: Themes of destruction of illusions, upheaval, chaos, sudden change, resilience, and rebuilding emerge.

Plot: The plot may involve disaster and sudden seismic shifts, with old constructs crumbling down and the need to dismantle outdated systems and rebuild.

Potential Story Conflict: Potential story conflicts include chaos following false stability, lasting repercussions, difficulty moving on after a traumatic experience, power struggles, and identity crises after loss.

Potential Relationship Conflict: In relationships, conflicts might involve betrayal, traumatic breakups, separation during or after a crisis, seeking support from outsiders, blaming each other, denial, and pushing each other's buttons.

17 - THE STAR

Basic Meaning: Represents hope, faith, purpose, and renewal.

Character: Depicts a character who is optimistic, abundant, serene, intuitive, inspired, and creative.

Traits and archetypes the Star card could reflect: A character who embodies the Star card is imbued with hope and renewal. They may also serve as a north star or guiding light, and be a dreamer, healer, light-bearer, muse, map-maker, or visionary.

Potential Positive Traits: This character finds silver linings and blessings in disguise. They're adept at maintaining perspective and stride towards their dreams. Star characters tend to be resilient, willing to be vulnerable, and open to new paths forward. Their intuitive nature serves as a calming and uplifting force for others.

Potential Shadow Traits: Star characters may also exhibit shadow traits such as being unrealistic, trapped in delusions, ignoring problems and pain, detaching when faced with difficulty, being dreamers who don't put plans into action, ignoring intuition, or displaying toxic positivity.

Themes: Themes may involve finding hope again in challenging times, renewing faith in brighter days ahead, the power of resilience and perseverance, and cautionary tales of unintended consequences.

Plot: The story may revolve around a journey of renewal and hope following a period of hardship. It explores how guidance and a stroke of luck can pave the way forward after tragedy strikes, ultimately leading to a reconciliation over lost faith.

Potential Story Conflict: The protagonist's naiveté and overly optimistic outlook may lead to unrealistic expectations and missed opportunities. There's a tension between hopeful optimism and the harsh realities of taking action and facing the consequences of one's choices.

Potential Relationship Conflict: As the characters evolve, they may outgrow certain situations and relationships. Conflicts could also surface from a failure to address underlying problems or avoiding difficulties.

18 - THE MOON

Basic Meaning: Represents illusion, fear, anxiety, and the subconscious.

Character: Depicts a character who is dreamy, mysterious, malleable, otherworldly, intuitive, or grappling with misinformation and fear.

Traits and archetypes the Moon card could reflect: The character may be a dreamer, mystic, lunar priestess, dream walker, shape-shifter, or creature of the night. Characters governed by Moon energy might be dual-natured, nocturnal, or confronted by illusions.

Potential Positive Traits: This character is imaginative, creative, and able to access deeper truths beyond the veil of consciousness. They may be open to navigating ambiguity and gray areas, receptive to intuition and the subconscious, and have senses attuned to things that lay beyond the rational mind. Moon characters may explore their shadows constructively.

Potential Shadow Traits: This character can also be fearful, paranoid, and manipulative. They may use misdirection, get lost in illusions, or ignore reality. They could also wrestle with anxiety, crippling doubts. and be overly sensitive to slights. Some may feel uncomfortable with the unknown and/or the supernatural.

Themes: Themes could involve unveiling inner shadows, confronting hidden aspects of oneself, navigating illusion and deception, or discovering that appearances can be deceiving.

Plot: The story may center around unraveling the truth behind facades, the struggle between intuition and illusion, or exposing secrets concealed beneath a glossy surface.

Potential Story Conflict: In the story, characters may battle paranoia or confront worst-case scenarios. They could grapple with confronting buried worries and emotions or other inner conflicts and revelations, perhaps discovering unsettling truths about a loved one.

Potential Relationship Conflict: Relationships could be tested when dealing with misunderstandings or distorted perceptions, reluctance to see beyond surface appearances, self-sabotage fueled by crippling doubts, or withdrawing from relationships out of fear.

19 - The Sun

Basic Meaning: Represents positivity, success, and vitality.

Character: Depicts a character who is playful, confident, radiating positivity and energy.

Traits and archetypes the Sun card could reflect: A character inspired by the Sun card reflects joy and vitality. This person is a creator, full of life force. This character could also be a child or character who retains a youthful exuberance or sense of wonder. They may be a golden boy or girl, who inspires others.

Potential Positive Traits: This character radiates joy and vitality, exhibits a vivacious and healthy demeanor, abundant in energy. They uplift others' spirits through open-hearted generosity, with a zest for life that promotes growth and sparks passion. This person shines their light on others with a realistic yet buoyant view point, brimming with natural talents.

Potential Shadow Traits: This character can also be naïve, prone to excess, or oblivious to others' difficulties. They may expect constant rewards and adulation, or be resentful of limitations. When faced with disappointment, they can be petulant and childish. They're prone to developing indulgent habits or hogging the spotlight.

Themes: Themes revolve around hope and faith that better times will come. Other potential themes include cycles of joy and sadness, and healing after the passage of time.

Plot: Success and joy come easily, but is this too good to be true?

Potential Story Conflict: Characters' blind spots and avoidance of problems can cause tension, as can the pressure to maintain constant cheerfulness. Characters may also struggle to live up to an idealized image.

Potential Relationship Conflict: Egos clash and competition arises. A character does *not* want to be someone's manic pixie dream girl. The gap between toxic positivity and realism causes strife. A grumpy/sunshine romantic pairing clashes over outlook on life. Obliviousness to the pain of others or excessive indulgence causes friction or blindness to troubles.

20 - JUDGMENT

Basic Meaning: Signifies rebirth, awakening, and absolution.

Character: This character stands at a crossroads. They may have an awakening and gain new perspective, or feel drawn towards a higher calling.

Traits and archetypes the Judgment card could reflect: This character carries rebirth energy. This could take the form of them undergoing a personal awakening or ushering in a rebirth for another person or group. They may serve as a reformer, crusader, baptizer, or herald of something new.

Potential Positive Traits: This character has evolved and entered a state where they can learn from the past and use lessons to make progress. They may inspire positive change in others. They're able to self-reflect with grace and honesty, find renewed purpose, be transformed by revelations, awakened to higher truths, and possess a transparent and reborn spirit.

Potential Shadow Traits: Judgment characters can also become self-righteous, leading to harsh judgment of others without mercy to temper it. They may preach without practicing, or use awakening to gain status or followers. At one extreme, they may be excessively remorseful and at the other unforgiving. They could refuse to let go of past mistakes.

Themes: Themes revolve around absolution, forgiveness, self-forgiveness, radical life changes, evolution, or rebirth.

Plot: The story could center on second chances, pivotal decision points, resurrection, the struggle of reliving past errors, tough love, or intervention.

Potential Story Conflict: Conflicts may stem from repeating past mistakes a la *Ground Hog Day*, the challenge of learning and growing, or the deception of false prophets.

Potential Relationship Conflict: In interpersonal relationships, conflicts spring from grudges, the struggle to forgive and move forward, discrepancies in reaching goals or positive states of being, feelings of being left behind, or the denial of one's true nature hindering complete love.

21 - THE WORLD

Basic Meaning: Signifies completion, success, and wholeness.

Character: Depicts a character who is fulfilled, whole, with a unity of self and purpose.

Traits and archetypes the World card could reflect: A World card character radiates wholeness and completion. The character represented by this card may be a traveler, seeker, chronicler, life-long learner, or master with a global perspective. They have achieved integration, mastery over at least one area of study or life.

Potential Positive Traits: This character integrates lessons into wisdom, embraces the joyous flow of life, and appreciates life's richness and paradoxes fully. They've found balance, returned with the elixir and leave a legacy through contributions. This is someone who has leveled-up. They've reconciled the disparate parts of themselves and reached a point of acceptance and integration of all they've experienced.

Potential Shadow Traits: This character may stagnate after a cycle of growth, prone to settling back into comfort and routine. If they get complacent, they'll miss the value of continual growth, hit plateaus, and stop going. Excessive self-indulgence after success can create problems. They may also become isolated because of a new higher status or title and overlook possibilities on the horizon for continued growth.

Themes: Themes center around fulfillment, accomplishment, good triumphing over evil, wholeness, integration of all parts of self, or the risks of complacency.

Plot: The story leads to a culmination of a character's journey, ultimately achieving wholeness, or attaining a new level of understanding. A character could also experience stagnation and fret that the best moments are in the past.

Potential Story Conflict: Characters face feeling aimless without further goals, losing a sense of purpose, negative changes after achieving success, or a myopic focus on details rather than the bigger picture.

Potential Relationship Conflict: Relationships come into conflict when characters drift apart, outgrow current circumstances, succumb to self-indulgence, or struggle with a difference in status.

CHAPTER 7.2

DECIPHERING THE MINOR ARCANA

The Minor Arcana is made up of four suits: Wands, Cups, Swords, and Pentacles (also known as Coins). Each suit contains fourteen cards: Ace through Ten cards, plus the four court cards: Page, Knight, Queen, and King.

While the Major Arcana symbolizes significant life events and lessons, the Minor Arcana reflects life's daily fluctuations and challenges.

CHAPTER 7.3

INTERPRETING THE MINOR ARCANA FOR STORY SPARKS: WANDS

WANDS (AKA RODS)

Element: Fire

Represents: Passion, creativity, action, inspiration, and purpose

Digging Deeper: The suit of Wands symbolizes the element of fire and embodies the energies of passion, inspiration, creativity, and action. Wands are associated with big ideas, drive, ambition, adventure, and starting new projects or journeys.

In terms of character archetypes, Wands cards could represent creators, visionaries, explorers, entrepreneurs, performers, or leaders who are vibrant, energetic, and charismatic. Protagonists aligned with Wands may be spontaneous, enthusiastic, and bold.

For plot and narrative arcs, the suit of Wands may evoke themes of creation, exploration, risk-taking, pursuing dreams or callings, or overcoming challenges with determination. Wands might signify a character going on a quest or journey, chasing inspiration, discovering passion, or transforming ideas into action.

Stories exploring Wands' energy may feature twists, surprises, and unexpected developments that drive the narrative forward.

In this section, we'll examine each card in the suit of Wands, its basic meaning and discuss potential interpretations based on character, theme, plot, potential story conflict, and potential relationship conflict.

ACE OF WANDS

Basic Meaning: Symbolizes new creative inspirations, igniting passions, and bringing fresh energy, vitality, and enthusiasm.

Character: Depicts a character who is a visionary, inspired artist, idealist, pioneer, or budding entrepreneur.

Positive Traits: This character could be creative, inspired, or excited by possibilities. They're curious and eager to learn, take initiative on inspiration. They are action-oriented and willing to work hard toward goals.

Shadow Traits: This character could also struggle with follow-through. Passions may burn bright but briefly for this individual, who is easily distracted by shiny new things and prone to bite off more than they can chew.

Themes: Potential themes include the importance of hard work to realize dreams, understanding that passion requires follow-through to make an impact, or the ability to inspire others.

Plot: The plot may revolve around a new opportunity, a call to adventure, a surge of inspiration, or perhaps a divide due to good intentions lacking follow-through. It could also involve creative blocks, experiencing moments of magic, manifestation of creative gifts, or a fire starting.

Potential Story Conflict: Story conflicts may include challenges in finding inspiration or focusing creative energy effectively. In addition, someone with good intentions might not manifest them into real accomplishments.

Potential Relationship Conflict: Tension arises from disagreements over pursuing a new idea or passion, frustration over a partner's pile of abandoned projects, neglect of intimacy because of an obsessive focus on other passions, or experiencing burnout and withdrawal after a period of intense creativity.

TWO OF WANDS

Basic Meaning: Signifies planning, exploration, assessing possibilities, envisioning goals, worldly aspirations, and big-picture thinking.

Character: Depicts a character who's an explorer, entrepreneur, architect, world traveler, or futurist.

Positive Traits: This character may exhibit strategic and organized thinking. They're ambitious, goal-oriented, and often inspire others with their vision. They have a knack for balancing long-term and short-term goals, and possess a commanding presence.

Shadow Traits: This character may also make lofty plans without taking action. They could lose sight of present needs because of long-term thinking, neglect to account for obstacles, or set unrealistic time lines and expectations. They could also fall prey to hubris or arrogance about their vision.

Themes: Themes revolve around making decisions, visualizing the future, and making amends for past mistakes.

Plot: The plot could involve laying out goals, encountering unforeseen challenges, balancing planning with passion, and charting direction through strategy and innovation.

Potential Story Conflict: Conflicts could stem from plans going awry, fear about taking the next step, goals proving unrealistic, or possessing vision but lacking practical consideration.

Potential Relationship Conflict: Relationship conflicts could arise from differing visions of the future, conflict over travel styles, delays, and the tension between comfort and adventure.

THREE OF WANDS

Basic Meaning: Represents teamwork, collaboration, delegation, expanding operations, progress, and confidence in a solid strategy to move forward.

Character: Depicts a character who's an ambassador, project manager, matchmaker, community organizer, or liaison.

Positive Traits: This character demonstrates dependability and support for others, brings people together around shared goals, values diversity of perspective, shares the workload, and serves as an effective team player and leader.

Shadow Traits: This character may also take credit for others' work, exhibit poor management or micro-management tendencies. They could also over-extend without considering limits, fail to give autonomy or feedback, or adopt an "I work alone" mentality.

Themes: Themes center around expanding horizons, taking initiative, community building, and working toward a shared vision.

Plot: In the plot, a group of individuals may come together around a shared goal or vision, relying on each other for safety in treacherous situations. Narratives could also include characters encountering cliques or facing corporate sabotage.

Potential Story Conflict: Conflict comes from poor team dynamics, over-expansion, and uncertainty about who to trust on one's team. Other sources of conflict include backstabbing in a professional situation, or fear of trust.

Potential Relationship Conflict: Disagreements may crop up over decisions about which risks to take, micro-management, hogging credit, undermining partnerships or teams for personal gain, or friction because of unequal distribution of work.

FOUR OF WANDS

Basic Meaning: Symbolizes celebration, achievement of goals, happiness, stability, and the importance of making time to acknowledge and toast to accomplishments.

Character: Depicts a character who's a host, party of event planner, homemaker, peacekeeper, traditionalist, or family anchor.

Positive Traits: This character appreciates life's blessings and offers stability and support to others. They work diligently and enjoy the fruits of their labor. They also value community and traditions, maintain an optimistic outlook, and find joy in simple pleasures.

Shadow Traits: This character may become materialistic and driven by status. They could grow complacent after a period of success, resist growth or change, or miss opportunities due to preserving routine. They could also resist facing problems to maintain the status quo, or grow dependent on the approval or praise of others.

Themes: Themes include marking milestones, excitement over progress, celebrations, and marriage.

Plot: Plot events may center around a significant achievement, a reason for celebration, or starting a journey into a new phase of life.

Potential Story Conflict: Conflicts arise from a celebration that is premature or short-lived, public attention and facing criticism or danger due to newfound status, letting fame inflate one's ego, or succumbing to materialism or status-obsession.

Potential Relationship Conflict: Relationship rifts may bubble up due to jealousy over accomplishments, suppressing feelings to keep the peace, differing celebration styles (one preferring extravagance while the other likes to keep it low-key), or comparisonitis.

FIVE OF WANDS

Basic Meaning: Represents competition, rivalry, petty disagreements, and struggles.

Character: Depicts a character who is a competitor, debater, revolutionary, firestarter, or prankster.

Positive Traits: This character is driven to improve through challenges, thrives in high-pressure situations, learns from both victories and losses, motivates others through example, and remains competitive yet gracious.

Shadow Traits: This person could also exhibit poor sportsmanship when losing, hold grudges or refuse to compromise. They may seek out conflict for its own sake, sow discord and divisiveness, or need to prove themselves at others' expense.

Themes: Themes could revolve around strife, tension, rivalry, and viewing struggle as an opportunity to rise to the occasion.

Plot: The plot may feature many obstacles arising, in-fighting occurring, or competition turning toxic. The stakes may escalate to life-and-death. Unfair advantages complicate situations, or characters engage in verbal sparring.

Potential Story Conflict: Conflicts pop up when competition turns destructive rather than motivational or grudges spur people to take dangerous actions.

Potential Relationship Conflict: Conflicts may involve vying for dominance in a relationship, engaging in one-upmanship, one person constantly instigating conflict, or two people being on opposite sides of a conflict.

SIX OF WANDS

Basic Meaning: Represents victory, success, triumph over obstacles, public recognition, and feeling confident because of accomplishments.

Character: Depicts a character who is a hero, heroine, star performer, inspiring leader, champion, or trailblazer.

Positive Traits: This character is victorious, self-assured, charismatic, and maintains their work ethic despite accolades. They set healthy standards of excellence, celebrate wins with humility and gratitude, and inspire others, leading by example and sharing credit.

Shadow Traits: This character may also tend toward arrogant and boastful behavior, becoming entitled and ceasing to grow after recognition. They may rest on past laurels with smug satisfaction and take credit at the expense of their teammates.

Themes: Themes include public recognition, heroism, praise, or dealing with being in the public eye.

Plot: Plot events could involve triumph after struggle, gaining admiration, or perhaps someone steals credit from another.

Potential Story Conflict: A victor may grow arrogant, with success isolating them. They may experience anxiety about future performance and doubts about measuring up to past success.

Potential Relationship Conflict: Relationship tensions arise over feeling jealous of someone else's success, having an obsessive need for praise and reassurance, or getting too comfortable.

SEVEN OF WANDS

Basic Meaning: Represents defending principles, standing your ground, facing challenges, fortitude, courage, and protectiveness.

Character: Depicts a character who's a guardian, sentinel, hilltop defender, last stand warrior, or resolute leader.

Positive Traits: This character leads by example, showing strength and grit. They stand up for principles with integrity, seeking non-violent solutions whenever possible. They inspire others through determination and are flexible, willing to compromise if necessary.

Shadow Traits: However, they can be defensive and unwavering, sometimes becoming combative and confrontational. They may lack flexibility and refuse help or new perspectives. Their aggression might be the first response rather than a last resort, and they can display stubbornness.

Themes: The themes revolve around perseverance, determination, and standing up for what's right despite the cost.

Plot: The plot involves withstanding challenges, refusing to back down, engaging in negotiations, and advocating for justice.

Potential Story Conflict: Conflict arises when principles are taken too far, leading to unwillingness to compromise. The character may face attacks from detractors and battle inner demons.

Potential Relationship Conflict: Stubbornness can prevent understanding and compromise in relationships. There may be a conflict between integrity and the detrimental consequences of actions, as well as clashes of ego.

Eight of Wands

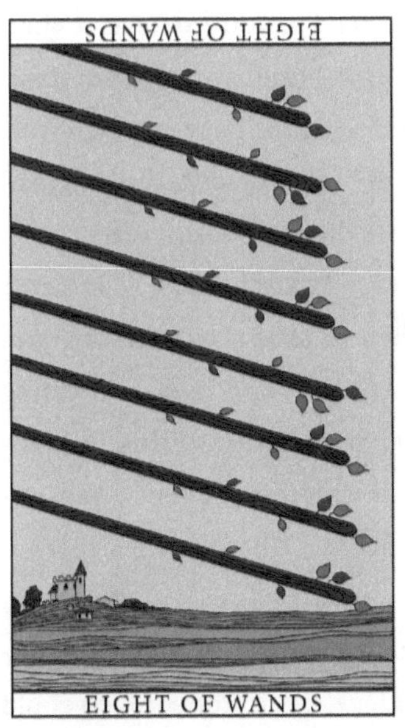

Basic Meaning: Symbolizes swift progress, rapid communication, travel, movement, and forward momentum.

Character: Depicts a character who is a messenger, courier, entrepreneur, or fast-track achiever.

Positive Traits: This character makes quick decisions when necessary and thrives in environments with variety and change. They motivate others with their energy and are adaptable and flexible thinkers. This character brings a fresh perspective to challenges and embraces opportunities with versatility and speed.

Shadow Traits: However, they may be prone to rushing without planning and resist stability or commitment. They might have trouble weighing the risks of impulsive actions, appearing flighty, scattered, or restless.

Themes: The themes revolve around swift change and forward motion.

Plot: The plot involves a whirlwind of activity and fast-paced developments, often featuring impulsively accepting an opportunity.

Potential Story Conflict: Conflict arises when moving too fast leads to carelessness, or when rapid movement causes overwhelm and panic.

Potential Relationship Conflict: In relationships, there might be a failure to commit time, restlessness, and impulsive acts, risking security and safety.

NINE OF WANDS

Basic Meaning: Represents perseverance, resilience, guarding accomplishments, being wary, finishing energy, or completion of an arduous task.

Character: This card depicts a character who is a sentinel, scarred survivor, or hardened veteran. They may be a stoic sage, or soul healer, described as exhausted but unyielding, or world-weary.

Positive Traits: This character knows when to retreat to gain strength, and is determined and tireless in facing challenges. Stoic and inspiring in hardship, they maintain a prudent defensiveness without hostility, and learn from setbacks.

Shadow Traits: However, this character may become paranoid and distrustful, refusing new opportunities out of fatigue. Their stubbornness could prolong recovery, and defensiveness could escalate to aggression. They often struggle to ask for help or admit weakness.

Themes: Persistence through hardship and survival are central themes.

Plot: Plots inspired by this card often involve a character's resolve enduring despite setbacks. They may be recovering from the horrors of war or another catastrophic event, learning to trust again after trauma, or preparing for the final push toward their goal.

Potential Story Conflict: Conflict arises when stubbornness prevents necessary course corrections, when a character stays stuck instead of moving forward, or when excessive vigilance hinders progress.

Potential Relationship Conflict: In relationships, refusing help or support, guardedness, and mentally fighting old battles can push others away and create conflict.

TEN OF WANDS

TEN OF WANDS

Basic Meaning: Represents responsibility, burden, struggle under the weight of commitments, or proximity to a successful outcome.

Character: Depicts a character who's a caregiver, martyr, or responsible sibling. This may be a steadfast public servant, often overloaded with responsibilities.

Positive Traits: They willingly shoulder the weight to help others and know when to lighten the load. Finding purpose in hard work, they're organized and seek help when needed. Despite challenges, they push through and carry out duties before resting, learning from each experience.

Shadow Traits: However, they may take on more than they can sustain alone and refuse help out of sheer willfulness. These tendencies risk the onset of burnout without rest or play, or lead to resentment towards their responsibilities. They may become consumed with work, neglecting their well-being.

Themes: The overarching themes include burden, burnout, and duty.

Plot: In the plot, ambition may backfire, leading to too much responsibility and harsh conditions.

Potential Story Conflict: Conflict builds when characters break under the workload, neglect their duties, or refuse help despite being overwhelmed. The narrative might also involve dragging out a situation that is ready to conclude, or when a fiercely dutiful provider is injured and forced to accept help.

Potential Relationship Conflict: In relationships, neglecting the needs of loved ones, harboring resentment due to burdens, and unwillingness to ask for help can create conflict.

PAGE OF WANDS

Basic Meaning: Signifies curiosity, enthusiasm, youthful energy, spark, spunk, exploration, new experiences, and spontaneity.

Character: Depicts a character who is a young explorer, inquisitive student, budding artist, adventurous child, or Energizer Bunny.

Positive Traits: The character is energetic and eager to learn and try new things. They openly chase their passions and are adaptable to changes in people and places. They motivate others through the joy of discovery, bringing fresh perspective and optimism. Their willingness to grow is a key trait.

Shadow Traits: However, they may take risks without considering safety and easily get distracted, losing focus. They might also be prone to bright passions that fade quickly, interrupt or ignore others' needs, and their impulsive actions may lack forethought.

Themes: Exploration, optimism, and taking chances are prominent themes.

Plot: The plot may involve a new journey or relationship beginning, or a new hobby leading to a potential love interest.

Potential Story Conflict: Conflict arises when lack of focus or maturity backfires, or when impulsive choices create risks and unintended consequences.

Potential Relationship Conflict: In relationships, impatience can strain bonds. Conflicts can spark from the dynamics of a grumpy/sunshine pairing, or there might be issues with entitled behavior due to lack of experience.

KNIGHT OF WANDS

Basic Meaning: Represents an adventurous spirit, passion, action, energy, initiative, restlessness, spontaneity, and channeling energy into purposeful action.

Character: Depicts a character who's a maverick, driven artist, entrepreneur, creative force, or passionate speaker.

Positive Traits: This character is daring and impulsive. They energize their team with enthusiasm and thrive under the pressure of tight deadlines. They're often dynamic go-getters who relish tackling new challenges. Through their bold vision and effort, they can inspire and motivate others.

Shadow Traits: However, their focus can be scattered by every shiny new thing, risking half-finished work or abandoned projects. Their charisma might mask disorganization and flakiness, and their restlessness can leave messes for others to clean up. There's also a risk of burnout because of an unsustainable pace.

Themes: Themes include adventure, confidence, passion, and making bold moves.

Plot: In the plot, the character charges ahead quickly, pursuing goals and leaping before looking.

Potential Story Conflict: Conflict takes form when impulsiveness leads to trouble or when distractions from "shiny object syndrome" hinder progress. Overconfidence can also create conflict.

Potential Relationship Conflict: In relationships, moving too fast, being unwilling to settle down, leaving a trail of messes, self-sabotage, and a lack of self-awareness can all lead to tension and conflict.

QUEEN OF WANDS

Basic Meaning: Represents boldness, capability, warmth, confidence, infectious energy, and a fiery yet pragmatic essence.

Character: Depicts a character who's a visionary matriarch, cultivator, and encourager with a warm heart. They're a cultivator of talent and an empowering force.

Positive Traits: A character represented by the Queen of Wands is generous with time, advice, and compliments. They're a natural leader who empowers others' gifts and remains calm under pressure. Through self-assurance, they cultivate teamwork through positivity and adapt nimbly to evolving circumstances.

Shadow Traits: However, they may be overly critical of themselves and others, stifling chances for growth. They might rely more on charm than merit to lead, and can be prone to flares of temper, defensiveness, and jealousy. There's a risk of this person becoming a demanding mentor due to pride, and expecting compliance over free expression.

Themes: Themes include vibrancy, determination, and balancing family and passions.

Plot: In the plot, the Queen of Wands may be leading others and catalyzing action.

Potential Story Conflict: Conflict may develop from a strained mentor/student dynamic, the expectation of compliance versus free expression, or disconnection stifling power.

Potential Relationship Conflict: In relationships, dominating partner dynamics, insecurity leading to undermining others to prop up a fragile ego, and defensiveness can all lead to conflict.

KING OF WANDS

Basic Meaning: Represents passionate, visionary leadership, a can-do spirit, risk taking, and an orientation toward action and determination.

Character: Depicts a character who's a visionary leader, bold entrepreneur, adventurer, inspirer, or trailblazer.

Positive Traits: This character is a prudent yet daring strategist, a pioneer, who inspires big dreams and perseverance. They lead boldly with integrity and wisdom, trusting and supporting their teammates' strengths. They adapt plans flexibly for new opportunities.

Shadow Traits: However, their charisma may mask gaps in preparation, and impatience with the process can risk instability. Overconfident plans might overlook realities, and an authoritarian approach may stifle collaboration. Their volatility can burn supporters through drama.

Themes: Themes include mastery, leadership, and inspiration.

Plot: In the plot, the character may face the final battle, seize authority, rally others, or make strategic plans.

Potential Story Conflict: Conflict arises from the abuse of power or unchecked ego.

Potential Relationship Conflict: In relationships, controlling behavior strains bonds. Volatility and risk-taking create conflict, and egomania can be detrimental.

INTERPRETING THE MINOR ARCANA FOR STORY SPARKS: CUPS

CUPS

Element: Water

Represents: emotion and relationships, intuition, and imagination.

Digging Deeper:

Cups represent the element of water in tarot, symbolizing emotions, relationships, creativity, and intuition. They touch upon themes of feelings, bonds, romance, artistry, and spirituality, reflecting the inner self.

Characters associated with Cups may be romantic, nurturing, empathetic, spiritual, artistic, or in touch with their dreams and fantasies. Cups-inspired protagonists could be healers, counselors, poets, musicians, or individuals in professions involving close interactions with others.

Narrative themes inspired by Cups could include romantic relationships, family ties, self-discovery, artistic expression, and emotional healing. Stories exploring vulnerability, openness, compassion, and emotional cycles may resonate with this suit.

When a Cups card is drawn to help with a story question, you may want to explore deep connections, or romantic interludes between characters. Cups cards can also pertain to tapping into creativity, understanding emotions, addressing relationships, creative blocks, following intuition, or profound inner transformation. The watery nature of Cups flows into imaginative storytelling and introspection.

ACE OF CUPS

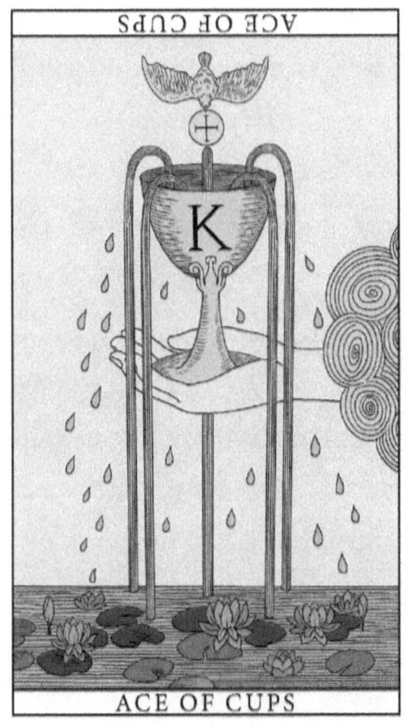

Basic Meaning: Represents new beginnings, creativity, inspiration, and spirituality. It signifies taking a plunge into new opportunities.

Character: Portrays a character who's an artist, caretaker, healer, inspiring friend, or spiritual guide.

Positive Traits: This character may express inner depths through creative outlets, foster meaningful connections, uplift others with care, or offer intuitive emotional insight.

Shadow Traits: This character may become overly emotional, dependent, or smothering. They're prone to taking on others' emotions and being disconnected from their own wants and needs. They could struggle with boundaries, or manipulate with tears.

Themes: Themes could include new beginnings, emotional renewal, embracing a new phase of life, or awakening joy.

Plot: The plot might involve a new relationship or emotional journey, starting a new life stage, or starting fresh after loss or divorce.

Story Conflict: Conflicts may spring from struggles with accepting new emotions or relationships, feeling out of one's depth in a new endeavor, or repressing emotions in a budding relationship.

Relationship Conflict: Interpersonal conflict can come from navigating the initial stages of a relationship, possibly coming to terms with hesitations or vulnerabilities.

TWO OF CUPS

Basic Meaning: Represents love, collaboration, and building emotional connections through partnerships and commitment.

Character: Depicts a character who plays the role of a soul mate, trusted confidante, team builder, understanding ally, or kindred spirit.

Positive Traits: This character leads with empathy and displays patience, commitment, and kindness. They may find fulfillment through supporting a partner's happiness. They value equality, sincerity, and compromise, supporting teammate's dreams and fostering healthy bonds. They recognize the worth of healthy interdependence.

Shadow Traits: However, this character may struggle with co-dependency, loss of individuality, or passive enablement of dysfunction. They may compromise too much at the expense of their own needs.

Themes: Themes include unity, partnership of equals, synergy, and not having to face things alone.

Plot: The plot may center on forming bonds or partnerships, possibly romantic in nature.

Story Conflict: Conflicts revolve around balancing new relationships with personal goals or fears, or navigating obstacles like star-crossed lovers or conflicting priorities.

Relationship Conflict: Relationship conflicts could center on managing early stages of deepening bonds, overcoming feelings of unworthiness, or reconciling social class differences.

THREE OF CUPS

Basic Meaning: Represents celebration, joy, and female camaraderie, emphasizing creative collaboration and friendship.

Character: Depicts a character who's a social butterfly, party planner, fun friend, creative networker, or community weaver.

Positive Traits: This character is social and joyful, adept at celebrating achievements and bringing people together. They enliven the social scene with their warmth and humor, and they value creating memorable moments and nurturing friendships through shared fun and inclusive event planning.

Shadow Traits: They may also struggle with overindulgence, avoidance of problems, or seeking validation at others' expense. They need to guard against envy and dependency on others' approval.

Themes: Themes focus on friendship, community, collaborative efforts, and supporting one another.

Plot: Plots can involve celebrations or gatherings that bring characters together, such as social events or party planning.

Story Conflict: Conflict may spring from challenges like overindulgence, distractions from important matters, or feeling excluded.

Relationship Conflict: Interpersonal conflicts likely address issues within friendships or community dynamics, such as lack of depth or inclusiveness, cliquishness, or dependence on others' approval.

FOUR OF CUPS

Basic Meaning: Represents emotional detachment, a sense of stability that paradoxically leads to boredom, indifference, and a disconnection from meaningful engagement, often resulting in missed opportunities.

Character: Depicts a character who's cynical, jaded, disillusioned, or who's hit a plateau.

Positive Traits: These characters are typically stable, with ready access to resources and opportunities, suggesting a solid foundation.

Shadow Traits: However, they may exhibit discontent, apathy, or a lack of gratitude. Their apparent laziness often hides a deeper fear of change, while their sullen attitude may conceal passive-aggressive tendencies. Stuck in a victim mentality, they may resent others' advantages, with their withdrawal indicating a deeper avoidance of engagement and isolation.

Themes: The primary themes include apathy, contemplation, and stagnation.

Plot: The narrative might explore a period of introspection or dissatisfaction, highlighting a character's journey through feelings of disengagement or disenchantment.

Story Conflict: The core conflict involves an internal struggle with unfulfilled desires or the realization of missed opportunities, challenging characters to confront their detachment.

Relationship Conflict: Relationship conflict grows from emotional withdrawal or disconnection within relationships, where characters may take others for granted.

FIVE OF CUPS

Basic Meaning: Represents loss, grief, sadness, regret, focusing on the past, loneliness, release, or a broken heart.

Character: Depicts a character who's a teacher of hard lessons, a mourner, comforter, resilient survivor, or phoenix rising.

Positive Traits: This character is deeply sensitive and possesses a profound emotional depth. They exhibit resilience, maintain hope through sadness, offer support during tough times, value lessons learned from difficult experiences, and extract wisdom from life's trials.

Shadow Traits: On the flip side, they might struggle with pessimism, remain fixated on the past, and find it hard to move forward. They might wait for others to fix their emotional issues, dwell on disappointments, project blame to avoid personal responsibility, and let withdrawal and cynicism overshadow their innate resilience.

Themes: Central themes revolve around the process of mourning, experiencing regret, and finding new perspectives through loss.

Plot: Stories may explore a character's loss or setback, the struggle with regret, or the challenge of moving beyond past sorrows.

Potential Story Conflict: Characters might grapple with releasing the past, overcoming grief, and embracing the lessons learned from their experiences.

Potential Relationship Conflict: Narratives could focus on the aftermath of a lost relationship or missed opportunity, highlighting the need to process and move beyond grief.

SIX OF CUPS

Basic Meaning: Represents nostalgia, childhood, memories, innocence, and joyful recollections.

Character: Depicts a character who's a keeper of traditions, eternal student, sentimentalist, or caregiver.

Positive Traits: Six of Cups characters are often nostalgic, and exude innocence and generosity. They place high value on family and community connections. They show empathy for others' vulnerabilities, find joy in learning from past experiences, and appreciate cherished memories.

Shadow Traits: However, they might be naïve, overly fixated on the past, and resistant to maturing. They tend to dodge current responsibilities, express resentment towards changes that challenge their childlike view of the world. Their rose-colored glasses vision of childhood could lead to neglecting the responsibilities and growth opportunities of adulthood.

Themes: Themes include the pull of nostalgia and the impact of past experiences on the present.

Plot: Narratives might feature characters revisiting places from their childhood, returning to a state of innocence, or rekindling connections with individuals from their past.

Story Conflict: Key conflicts involve characters grappling with their attachment to the past or the challenge of maturing and moving forward.

Relationship Conflict: Stories may explore rekindled relationships with former loves or childhood companions, or the process of confronting and accepting long-buried memories.

SEVEN OF CUPS

Basic Meaning: Represents illusions, the realm of imagination, creativity, and the lure of wishful thinking, alongside the challenges posed by having too many choices or distractions, and the inherent potential within.

Character: Depicts a character who's an artist, daydreamer, creative mind, muse, or storyteller. This is someone with great potential and resources at their disposal.

Positive Traits: These characters are marked by their vivid imagination, hopeful outlook, and playful engagement with the unusual and unexplored. They approach life as an endless quest for utopian dreams, brimming with innovative and bold ideas.

Shadow Traits: However, they can also be delusional, struggle with indecisiveness, prone to escaping reality, and indulge excessively in pleasures without considering the consequences.

Themes: The narrative may explore the concepts of choice and the deceiving nature of illusions.

Plot: The plot may involve confrontation, with multiple paths or decisions. Alternately, a character may fear making a bad choice.

Story Conflict: Characters grapple with losing their grip on reality, setting unattainable goals, or becoming paralyzed by over-analysis.

Relationship Conflict: These narratives often delve into the turmoil of relationships marred by uncertainty, indecision, or broken promises.

EIGHT OF CUPS

Basic Meaning: Represents recognizing sunk costs, strategic quitting, withdrawal, retreat, emotional detachment, and letting go.

Character: Depicts a character who's a seeker, explorer, guide, or a person on a quest for deeper meaning.

Positive Traits: This character is self-aware enough to course correct as needed, and good at knowing when to move on to find something better. They're open to new experiences and help others see the value in changing paths, too. They're always searching for what truly matters in life.

Shadow Traits: This character may abandon commitments too quickly, or avoid facing problems directly, using their quest to escape responsibilities.

Themes: Themes revolve around the ideas of starting anew, leaving behind what no longer serves us, or the journey of discovering that some commitments, relationships, groups, or long-held dreams might not be right for us anymore.

Plot: The plot line may involve a character's quest to find something more meaningful, or a character leaving something behind despite a significant time and energy investment. This could be a profession, a relationship, a group, a work in progress, or a childhood dream that no longer serves.

Story Conflict: Characters could struggle with the decision to leave or move on.

Relationship Conflict: Relationship issues could spring from a decision to leave a relationship or situation that no longer serves. Conflicts could also arise from a change in relationship dynamic when one person quits a shared habit, pastime, or group while the other doesn't. For example, one person may quit drinking and the other feels left out. One friend or partner strikes out on an adventure while the other feels left behind. One person leaves a religious group, cult, or MLM and no longer relates to the people still there.

NINE OF CUPS

Basic Meaning: Represents fulfillment, appreciation, contentment, emotional satisfaction, and the challenges of having our desires fulfilled.

Character: Depicts a character who is a pleasure-seeker, a person who loves life, values the little things, and generously shares their happiness with others.

Positive Traits: This character finds joy in life's simple pleasures. They recognize and are thankful for life's blessings, and enjoy a low-stress life through balance.

Shadow Traits: However, there's a risk of becoming too comfortable or self-congratulatory, where entitlement might take the place of thankfulness. Their enjoyment of life can sometimes lead to laziness or indulgence.

Themes: The story explores achieving deep satisfaction and the realization of dreams or wishes.

Plot: The narrative follows the character as they achieve a deeply desired goal or indulge in a period focused on self-care and personal joy.

Story Conflict: The character faces the dilemma of potentially becoming too content, which might lead to a lack of motivation or growth.

Relationship Conflict: The story could delve into how getting everything one wants can impact relationships. A character might win the lottery or reach a higher echelon of status or fame, which complicates relationships.

TEN OF CUPS

Basic Meaning: Represents the importance of happiness, family bonds, and community harmony in fostering emotional abundance and well-being.

Character: Depicts a character who serves as the cornerstone of their family, preserving traditions and nurturing relationships.

Positive Traits: This character excels in building fulfilling relationships and maintaining emotional balance within their family. They create a loving and trusting environment, fostering a sense of belonging across generations. Additionally, they skillfully resolve conflicts to uphold harmony and unity.

Shadow Traits: However, there's a risk of setting overly high expectations or idealizing family life, which may lead to overlooking underlying problems. Sometimes, in an effort to maintain peace, they lose sight of their own needs or harbor hidden resentments beneath a compliant facade.

Themes: The story revolves around the themes of harmony within the family unit and pursuing familial happiness.

Plot: The narrative centers on the attainment of emotional and familial fulfillment, juxtaposed with the challenges of family dysfunction.

Story Conflict: The character faces external threats to family or community harmony, such as uprisings or civil unrest, which put their role as the family guardian to the test.

Relationship Conflict: The story could explore the struggles of maintaining or restoring balance in family or community relationships amidst conflict or upheaval.

PAGE OF CUPS

Basic Meaning: Represents exploring intuition, creativity, and the potential of naïve dreams, with a focus on observation and serendipity.

Character: This character is imaginative, intuitive, and open-hearted, always eager to learn and express themselves creatively. They bring joy to others through their playful insights and offer unwavering support to friends by understanding their truths.

Positive Traits: This character is creative, intuitive, and open-hearted. They may be receptive learners soaking up new perspectives or expressive artists. Their playful spirit uplifts others through their funny insights, and they often serve as supportive friends who see others' truths.

Shadow Traits: This person can also be immature, overly emotional, or unrealistic. They may manipulate emotions without care for impact. High sensitivity could feed inner turmoil. This person may people-please to earn fragile acceptance. Their unfocused dreaming could also hamper progress.

Themes: The story explores themes of creativity and emotional expression.

Plot: The narrative revolves around an unexpected emotional message or a new creative idea that sparks the character's journey.

Story Conflict: The character grapples with their own emotional maturity and expression, navigating the challenges that come with their sensitivity and idealistic nature.

Relationship Conflict: The story delves into the character's struggles with naivety and immaturity in handling relationships, as well as the doubts that arise from their high sensitivity.

KNIGHT OF CUPS

Basic Meaning: Represents someone who is a charming, romantic, idealistic lover, creative but somewhat flighty.

Character: Depicts a character who's a passionate wanderer, inspiring trailblazer, bold champion, risk-taking creative, or gallant defender.

Positive Traits: This character is charming, idealistic, and deeply passionate, approaching life with a bold and chivalrous spirit. They ardently pursue their passions while respecting the desires of others, serving as a valiant protector, and captivating those around them with their charismatic charm.

Shadow Traits: Their idealism can sometimes lead to moodiness and unrealistic expectations. Their charm might be perceived as manipulative, masking inner discontent or seeking attention. They may also engage in reckless behavior, endangering themselves or others for excitement, and their impulsivity may invite drama.

Themes: The story revolves around themes of romance and idealism, highlighting the allure of passionate pursuits.

Plot: The narrative follows the character's pursuit of a dream or romantic quest, driven by their adventurous spirit and idealistic nature.

Story Conflict: The character faces challenges in balancing their idealism with the realities of life, navigating the tension between their dreams and the practicalities of the world.

Relationship Conflict: The story explores the character's quest for a romantic or idealized relationship, possibly confronting disillusionment as they realize the difference between fantasy and reality. They may find themselves in love with the idea of love rather than the person themselves.

QUEEN OF CUPS

Basic Meaning: Represents a compassionate, motherly figure, nurturing, intuitive, and emotionally balanced.

Character: Depicts a character who is a nurturer, counselor, creative soul, or empath who offers guidance and support with warmth and understanding.

Positive Traits: This character is empathetic, nurturing, and emotionally stable, providing a comforting presence to those in need. They express their creativity as a way to process emotions and uplift themselves and others. Their guidance is thoughtful and balanced, helping people feel seen and understood.

Shadow Traits: However, they may struggle with sensitivity and moodiness, becoming absorbed in their emotions. Resentment can arise if their boundaries are not respected, leading to enabling behaviors or withholding care as a form of punishment.

Themes: The story explores themes of emotional security and intuition, highlighting the importance of nurturing relationships.

Plot: The narrative follows a character as they provide support and guidance to others.

Story Conflict: The character faces challenges in maintaining emotional boundaries and avoiding overextension, risking losing themselves in others' problems.

Relationship Conflict: The story delves into the character's struggle to balance emotional involvement with maintaining personal boundaries in their relationships.

KING OF CUPS

Basic Meaning: Represents a wise mentor with emotional intelligence who is cultured and mature in their feelings.

Character: Depicts a character who is a benevolent leader, diplomat, adviser, strategist, or peacekeeper.

Positive Traits: This character is emotionally balanced, diplomatic, and caring, with a deep capacity for empathy. They are devoted and loving partners who empower others through guidance and support. Their mastery of handling emotions allows them to navigate varied situations with skill, and their calm demeanor serves to defuse tensions strategically.

Shadow Traits: However, they may struggle with moments of manipulation or moodiness, harboring darker emotions beneath their composed exterior.

In vulnerable moments, they may withhold care as a means of asserting power, and their aloofness can sometimes mask a reluctance to confront their own feelings.

Themes: The story explores themes of emotional balance and wisdom, highlighting the importance of compassionate leadership.

Plot: The narrative may center on the character exercising compassionate leadership or making wise decisions, drawing on their emotional intelligence.

Story Conflict: The character faces challenges in maintaining emotional control or dealing with their own emotional struggles while fulfilling their leadership role.

Relationship Conflict: The story delves into the character's struggle to balance leading or guiding others with managing their personal emotions. Some may perceive their emotional intelligence as a weakness.

INTERPRETING THE MINOR ARCANA FOR STORY SPARKS: SWORDS

SWORDS

Element: Air

Represents: Intellect, logic, the realm of the mind, inner struggles, conflict, and mental health, along with communication.

Digging Deeper:

The suit of Swords embodies the element of air, symbolizing intellect, logic, truth, conflict, and effective communication. It encompasses ideals, beliefs, opinions, detachment, analysis, and clear mental focus.

Characters aligned with Swords may include scholars, strategists, lawyers, judges, writers, spokespeople, or activists focused on causes. They value justice, ethics, debate, and rigorous thinking.

Narrative themes inspired by Swords could include academic intrigues, battles of wit or ideals, ethical dilemmas, exposing corruption, fighting for justice, intellectual awakenings, or conflicts centered around beliefs. They often explore moral gray areas and struggles with issues like impostor syndrome, over-thinking, depression, or anxiety.

When a Swords card appears, it could inspire writing about seeking truth, overcoming confusion, dealing with conflict, articulating ideas, facing harsh realities, or using logic to cut through illusions. The double-edged nature of Swords can sharpen storytelling.

ACE OF SWORDS

Basic Meaning: Represents clarity, truth, mental acuity, sharp insights, breakthrough ideas, and the pursuit of justice.

Character: Depicts a character who's an inquirer in some capacity, a scholar, logician, advocate, or arbiter.

Positive Traits: This character is intellectually sharp, clear-minded, and truthful. They speak candidly with care, championing fair processes and equality. They use their intellect for justice and enlightenment, pursuing knowledge for growth and empowerment.

Shadow Traits: They may sometimes be overly critical or harsh, with a tendency to forget empathy in their pursuit of truth. They may use truth as a weapon rather than a tool for growth and wield facts to demean rather than engage in constructive debate.

Themes: Themes include new ideas, mental clarity, and mindset shifts.

Plot: The narrative may involve the revelation of truth or the start of a challenging journey, with a character experiencing a moment of clarity or breakthrough.

Story Conflict: The character faces struggles in cutting through confusion or deceit, confronting obstacles to uncovering the truth.

Relationship Conflict: A moment of truth can impact a relationship. Challenges can also spring from a character living too much in their head or differing perspectives.

TWO OF SWORDS

Basic Meaning: Represents indecision, lack of vision, avoidance, or being at an impasse.

Character: Depicts someone who's characterized by their diplomatic nature, yet prone to indecision and withdrawal when faced with difficult choices.

Positive Traits: This character is diplomatic, balanced, and thoughtful. They use stillness to listen deeply and reflect, seeking wise compromises by considering all perspectives. They mask their reactions to maintain calm under pressure and carefully weigh choices to minimize harm.

Shadow Traits: However, they can also be indecisive, avoidant, and in denial. They may procrastinate tough decisions, hindering progress, and frustrate others by being opaque or feigning neutrality to avoid taking responsibility.

Themes: Possible themes include indecision and balance.

Plot: The narrative may involve a character facing a difficult choice or dilemma, struggling with indecision or avoidance.

Story Conflict: The character experiences paralysis over a decision or denial of the truth, with their inaction becoming a passive decision in itself.

Relationship Conflict: The narrative may explore an impasse in communication or a relationship stalemate, where the characters are unwilling to confront problems or make necessary decisions.

THREE OF SWORDS

Basic Meaning: Represents heartbreak, grief, and separation, suggesting a period of emotional pain and sorrow.

Character: Depicts a person who's a survivor, characterized by their resilience and capacity to endure hardship, yet deeply affected by emotional wounds.

Positive Traits: This character is resilient, deeply feeling, and honest. They gain deeper wisdom from facing hard truths head-on, using their experiences of hurt to activate empathy and comfort others with compassion.

Shadow Traits: However, heartbreak takes its toll. This character can also be bitter or get stuck wallowing in pain. They may avoid taking responsibility for their healing, allowing bitterness to poison relationships and projecting their hurt outward as a shield. They may use pain to avoid confronting their true selves and shirk accountability.

Themes: Possible themes include sorrow, heartbreak, grief, and finding purpose through pain, suggesting the potential for growth and transformation in the face of adversity.

Plot: The narrative may involve an event causing deep emotional pain or betrayal, leading the character on a journey of healing and self-discovery.

Story Conflict: The character struggles to overcome grief or betrayal.

Relationship Conflict: The aftermath of betrayal or loss may lead to bitterness and conflict in relationships.

FOUR OF SWORDS

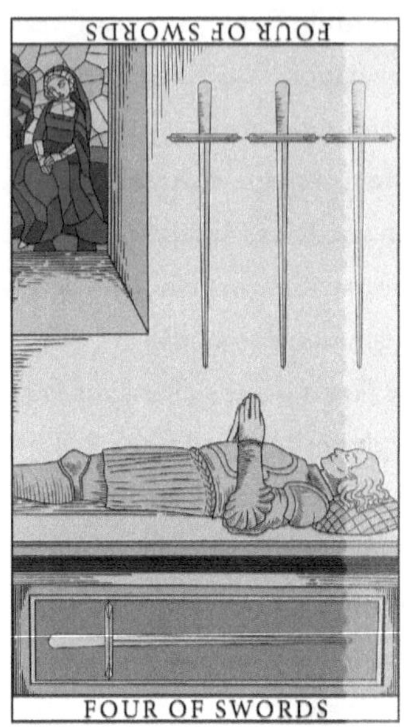

Basic Meaning: Represents rest, respite, and retreat, suggesting a period of recuperation after experiencing strife.

Character: Depicts one who's characterized by their contemplative nature and ability to find solace in solitude.

Positive Traits: This character is reflective, restful, and prepared. They use mindful solitude and respite to restore their energy and clarity, using quiet time productively for replenishment. They emerge from this period refreshed, with renewed clarity and perspective.

Shadow Traits: However, they can also be isolated, inactive, and disconnected. Their withdrawal may mask avoidance of responsibility, and isolation can breed resentment in the absence of interaction. Apathy may replace regained energy, and denying needed social supports can further exacerbate their struggles.

Themes: Possible themes include rest, contemplation

Plot: The narrative may involve a period of recovery or reflection after a conflict, as the character regroups and redirects their energies.

Story Conflict: A character confronts the need for healing from mental or physical exhaustion, navigating internal and external obstacles to find restoration.

Relationship Conflict: Withdrawal for self-care or healing may lead to conflict in relationships, as others struggle to understand their need for solitude or deal with their short fuse resulting from running on empty for too long.

FIVE OF SWORDS

Basic Meaning: Represents defeat, loss, conflict, and manipulation, suggesting a situation where winning may not feel like a victory. This card can also signify an unfair advantage, strategy, cruelty, and outwitting others.

Character: Depicts a character who's known for their competitive nature and strategic mindset, willing to do whatever it takes to come out on top. They thrive on rivalry and competition.

Positive Traits: This character is a strategic, resilient survivalist. They often win through skill and strategy rather than resorting to underhanded tactics.

Shadow Traits: However, they can also be unethical, spiteful, and overly competitive. They may gloat over others' losses and have a zero-sum game mentality.

Themes: Themes include conflict and unfair tactics.

Plot: The narrative may involve a conflict where winning is achieved through cheating or other dubious means, or a warning shot being fired.

Story Conflict: The character grapples with the consequences of their actions, facing internal and external conflicts as they prioritize short-term gains over long-term integrity.

Relationship Conflict: Discord and manipulation may arise in relationships, as the character exhibits an unhealthy need for dominance and control.

SIX OF SWORDS

Basic Meaning: Represents moving on, transition, and hope for the future, suggesting a journey away from troubles towards something better.

Character: Depicts an individual who's characterized by their ability to guide others through transitions and navigate towards a brighter future.

Positive Traits: This character is adaptable, hopeful, and rational. They focus on the promise ahead rather than dwelling on past worries, guiding the journey to a healthier destination with care and consideration.

Shadow Traits: However, they can also be detached and escapist, unwilling to confront the past. They may drag others along without fully understanding the costs, and their fixation on the past can make change disorienting without clear direction.

Themes: Possible themes include transition and moving on, highlighting the challenges and opportunities that come with leaving the past behind.

Plot: The narrative may involve a journey away from troubles towards something better.

Story Conflict: The character grapples with the challenges of leaving the past behind, navigating internal and external roadblocks as they strive for a brighter future.

Relationship Conflict: In relationships, conflicts may arise as the characters navigate difficult phases and struggle to find consensus about the way forward. Feelings of being left behind also cause strife.

SEVEN OF SWORDS

Basic Meaning: Represents acts of deception, dishonesty, and betrayal, coupled with the strategic thinking and trickery often employed for escape or outwitting opponents, all rooted in a desire for self-preservation.

Character: Depicts a character who's skilled in the art of deception and strategy. This character could be a morally gray rogue or a trickster.

Positive Traits: This character is marked by cleverness, strategic foresight, and an independent spirit. Their creativity and resourcefulness allow them to navigate and solve problems through unorthodox methods.

Shadow Traits: However, their darker aspects include a propensity for deceit, unreliability, and prioritizing self-interest. Their secretive nature and underhanded tactics can gradually undermine trust and goodwill, as they manipulate situations for personal gain.

Themes: Possible themes revolve around the dual nature of deception and strategic thinking.

Plot: The narrative may weave through tense scenarios of stealth, strategic escapes, or cunning plans, with the character employing their sharp wits to navigate complex situations.

Story Conflict: At the heart of the story lies a moral quandary, whether the ends justify the means and the ethical implications of relying on deceit and cunning as tools for survival or success.

Relationship Conflict: The character's journey is complicated by trust issues, stemming from their deceptive nature and selfish motivations.

EIGHT OF SWORDS

Basic Meaning: Represents feeling trapped, or being bound by restrictions or thoughts

Character: Depicts a character entangled in the web of their mental health challenges and intrusive thoughts, yet poised on the brink of self-discovery and liberation.

Positive Traits: Despite their constraints, this character is remarkably self-aware and possesses an underlying strength that propels them towards seeking freedom. They view their struggles as hurdles to be navigated, fostering a mindset geared towards problem-solving rather than resignation.

Shadow Traits: However, the shadow that looms large over them is a pervasive sense of victimhood and powerlessness. This crisis mindset transforms solvable problems into insurmountable obstacles, fostering a paralyzing identity rooted in fear, despair, and a stifling anxiety that obscures any potential paths forward.

Themes: The narrative threads together themes of psychological confinement, the battle with self-imposed limitations, and the quest for empowerment within the bounds of one's own mind.

Plot: The storyline unfolds around scenarios where the protagonist grapples with feelings of powerlessness and entrapment, highlighting their internal struggle against the chains of their own making.

Story Conflict: The core of the conflict is the character's tumultuous journey to break free from the mental and emotional restrictions that bind them, symbolizing a broader struggle for psychological liberation.

Relationship Conflict: Within the tapestry of human connections, the protagonist's sense of entrapment extends to their relationships, where they feel constricted and blinded to potential solutions.

NINE OF SWORDS

Basic Meaning: Represents a pervasive sense of unease, anxiety, worry, insomnia, mental anguish, and rumination.

Character: Depicts a character who's a sentinel on constant alert, wrestling with their instincts to foresee and forestall every conceivable danger. They embody the archetypal overthinker.

Positive Traits: Beneath their facade of fretfulness lies a deeply empathetic soul, keenly attuned to the consequences of actions. This relentless worry is not without merit. It propels them to meticulous planning and prevention, making them a guardian for others against unseen threats.

Shadow Traits: However, this incessant vigilance comes at a steep price: crippling anxiety, guilt, and an existence overshadowed by the specter of what could go wrong. Their life becomes a loop of ruminations that offer no exit, distorting relationships and turning existence into a series of problem-solving exercises devoid of joy.

Themes: Central themes include the pervasive grip of worry and guilt, the exhaustive cycle of rumination, and the protagonist's journey through their mental landscape marked by anxiety.

Plot: The storyline weaves through the protagonist's confrontation with their inner turmoil, a battle against their own mind's creations, seeking solace or understanding through therapy, self-reflection, or a pivotal life change.

Story Conflict: The narrative centers on the protagonist's struggle to navigate through their fears and to untangle the knots of past actions and their consequences.

Relationship Conflict: The protagonist's inner turmoil spills into their relationships, strained by misunderstandings born from unchecked worry and sleep-deprived irritability.

TEN OF SWORDS

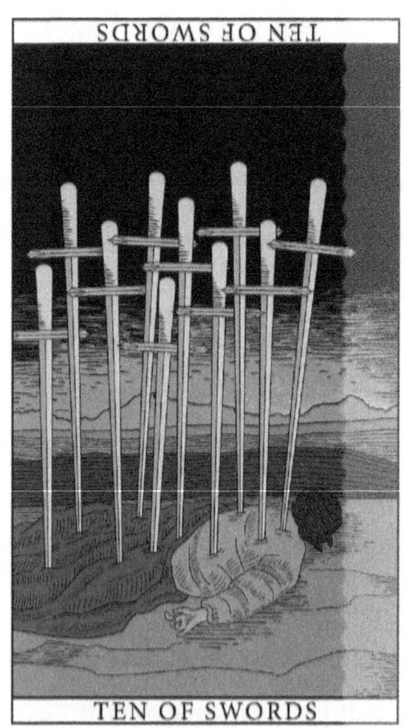

Basic Meaning: Represents finality, endings, painful conclusions, downfall, and rock bottom.

Character: Depicts a character who's a phoenix, a resilient spirit, downtrodden and defeated, but not done for yet.

Positive Traits: This character is marked by their ability to endure hardships and their acceptance of reality. They can surrender to learn rather than fight the inevitable, and see endings make way for new beginnings. They also find silver linings and hope even in total ruin.

Shadow Traits: This character is prone to catastrophizing and defeatist thinking. Fixating on feeling betrayed or wallowing in misery over losses denies their own power to shape what's ahead.

Themes: Possible themes include ruin, betrayal, and renewal after rock bottom.

Plot: In the story, a culmination of negative events leads to a dramatic conclusion, or a character faces a betrayal or a devastating end.

Story Conflict: A character must deal with the aftermath of a betrayal or loss.

Relationship Conflict: A severe betrayal puts a key relationship in jeopardy. Or when two characters end a relationship, this creates a tricky situation with mutual friends, who may feel like they have to choose sides.

PAGE OF SWORDS

Basic Meaning: Represents being inquisitive, intellectual, and quick-witted, and always ready to learn and solve puzzles.

Character: Depicts a character who's a student or amateur detective. They're curious, love to learn, and enjoy solving mysteries.

Positive Traits: This character is curious and loves to communicate. They're quick to learn and enjoy discussing ideas with others. They're good at seeing different perspectives and sharing what they know.

Shadow Traits: Sometimes they ask too many questions or gossip, which can make others uncomfortable. They might judge too quickly or use sarcasm in a way that wounds people instead of helping them.

Themes: The main themes are curiosity and exploration.

Plot: The story could involve discovering secrets or solving a mystery, maybe even going on a spy mission.

Story Conflict: The main challenge is dealing with immaturity and making responsible choices, especially when seeking knowledge or information.

Relationship Conflict: There might be misunderstandings or arguments because of poor communication or being judgmental.

KNIGHT OF SWORDS

Basic Meaning: Represents someone who's a swift thinker, prone to rash decisions, mental acuity, forward motion, and strategic thinking.

Character: They're a leader who gets things done, even if they're sometimes blunt. They're brave and protective of others.

Positive Traits: This character is full of energy and always ready to take action. They're smart and focused, charging ahead to achieve their goals. They decide quickly, which helps avoid delays. They protect others by planning ahead and communicating clearly.

Shadow Traits: Sometimes they act too quickly, without thinking, and can be aggressive or reckless. They may not consider how their actions affect others. They might talk too much and not listen enough, and their speeches can tire people out. They focus so much on efficiency that they forget about the human side of things.

Themes: Possible themes include bravery, and assertiveness, and the consequences of acting without forethought.

Plot: The story could involve a quick decision that leads to unexpected consequences, or a situation where impulsiveness causes problems.

Story Conflict: The main conflict comes from the fallout of a character's impulsive or aggressive actions.

Relationship Conflict: Characters might clash with others because of their impulsive or confrontational behavior.

QUEEN OF SWORDS

Basic Meaning: Represents someone clear-headed, perceptive, and wise.

Character: Depicts a character who's a counselor or mentor, offering insightful advice and seeing through to the heart of issues.

Positive Traits: This character is astute and good at explaining things clearly. They're independent and can see past facades to understand what's really going on. They're compassionate and fair, using reason to find truth without being harsh. They stand up for what's right and help those who need it.

Shadow Traits: Sometimes they appear cold or critical because they're detached from emotions. They might focus too much on planning and not enough on listening or working together with others.

Themes: Possible themes include clarity, independence, and strategy.

Plot: The story could involve making a clear decision or seeing through lies and illusions.

Story Conflict: Characters inspired by this card struggle to balance their clear thinking with empathy, sometimes coming off as too detached.

Relationship Conflict: Sharp intellect can create tension in relationships if a character comes across as arrogant or too focused on giving advice.

KING OF SWORDS

Basic Meaning: Represents someone who's a wise leader who values fairness and logic over emotions.

Character: Depicts a character who's a just ruler or a wise mentor, known for their fairness and strategic thinking.

Positive Traits: This character is wise and has authority. They're ethical and make decisions based on reason and compassion. They lead with a clear vision and inclusive planning, empowering their community.

Shadow Traits: Sometimes they can be rigid or cold because they focus too much on rules. They might micromanage or criticize too harshly, which can hurt others. Their detached leadership style might miss the emotions and needs of those they lead.

Themes: Possible themes include authority, ethical standards and relying on logic vs. emotion.

Plot: The story could involve making tough decisions that balance fairness and logic.

Story Conflict: Characters face challenges in upholding truth and justice in difficult situations.

Relationship Conflict: Characters struggle to maintain personal relationships while holding themselves and others to high standards, balancing their leadership responsibilities.

INTERPRETING THE MINOR ARCANA FOR STORY SPARKS: PENTACLES

PENTACLES (AKA COINS)

Element: Earth

Represents: This suit is grounded in the realm of the physical, tangible, and material. This includes work/ vocations, money, and physical health. Since this suit deals with the physical realm, it can be used to develop settings.

Digging Deeper: The suit of Pentacles represents the element of earth and the energy of the physical, material, and financial realms. Pentacles deal with prosperity, security, resources, possessions, work, health, and abundance.

Character archetypes aligned with Pentacles may be builders, business people, investors, craftspeople, or workers focused on tangible results and security. Protagonists could be pragmatic, hard-working, ambitious, and concerned with family or legacy.

Stories inspired by Pentacles could involve starting a business, achieving financial success, or coming into a windfall. They could also focus on craftsmanship, the discovery of hidden resources, rags-to-riches tales, or balancing work with health and family.

Drawing a Pentacles card could spark writing about establishing financial security, perhaps after a period of over-indulgence, budgeting, finding balance, valuing health, or appreciating simple things. Pentacles cards keep stories grounded and realistic.

ACE OF PENTACLES

Basic Meaning: Represents new opportunities, financial gain, material abundance, prospects, and seeds for success.

Character: Depicts a character who's good at making money and giving back. They might be a social entrepreneur, philanthropist, or conscientious steward.

Positive Traits: This character is always looking for new opportunities and avenues to success. They're practical, ambitious, and creative problem solvers. Their optimistic vision and pioneering spirit inspire others. Their stewardship protects resources for future prosperity.

Shadow Traits: However, they may also be materialistic, overly cautious, or greedy, hoarding benefits from others. They're also prone to boasting about success, and getting competitive.

Themes: Themes revolve around new opportunities, and the pros and cons of material success.

Plot: The story could kick off with someone starting a new business or finding a way to make money.

Story Conflict: The character's new opportunity or get-rich-quick scheme may come with unexpected or undesired consequences.

Relationship Conflict: Relationship conflicts could arise from adjusting to changes brought by new material circumstances. For example, winning the lottery or accepting a generous inheritance with strings attached could cause rifts.

TWO OF PENTACLES

Basic Meaning: Signifies juggling priorities, balancing multiple demands, resource management, and flexibility.

Character: Depicts a character who is a dynamic scheduler, flexible multitasker, project manager, event coordinator, or orchestra conductor.

Positive Traits: This character's great at adapting and can handle lots of tasks at the same time. They're resourceful, versatile, and can thrive even when things are uncertain. They help others by coordinating things well.

Shadow Traits: Sometimes, they take on too much and get overwhelmed. They might have trouble making decisions or end up doing things halfway because they're spread too thin. They might get stressed out when things don't go as planned.

Themes: Themes include finding balance and learning to be adaptable.

Plot: The story could involve someone trying to manage lots of tasks or dealing with pressure to perform well.

Story Conflict: The challenge might be figuring out how to keep everything in balance or making tough choices about what to prioritize.

Relationship Conflict: Relationships might suffer because your character is always busy with work or money issues. People might pressure them to take on too much.

THREE OF PENTACLES

Basic Meaning: Represents teamwork, craftsmanship, skill, professional accomplishments, and mastery.

Character: Depicts a character who's a humble perfectionist, a conscientious craftsperson, a team builder, or connector.

Positive Traits: This character is great at working with others and has high standards. They're dedicated and make sure even small tasks are done well. They bring people together, maximize the synergy of everyone's individual talents, and celebrate collective successes.

Shadow Traits: Sometimes this character can get overly focused on perfection. As a result, they can have a limited view of acceptable quality, and dismiss others' ideas. They can hog credit and diminish partners' worthy efforts. They can try to control everything, which smothers autonomy and innovation. At times, their high standards may be more about their ego than the actual work.

Themes: Themes revolve around collaboration, teamwork, and skill.

Plot: The story could be about people working together to achieve something, maybe in their jobs, and showing off their skills.

Story Conflict: The challenge might be finding a way to overcome obstacles as a team or using skills to solve a problem.

Relationship Conflict: There could be tension in working together, like professional jealousy or conflicts within the team.

FOUR OF PENTACLES

Basic Meaning: Represents being cautious with money and possessions, fearing loss and wanting to hold onto what you have.

Character: Depicts a character who is very careful with their money. They might be a miser, a conservative guardian, or a prudent strategist.

Positive Traits: This character is financially prudent, stable, and security-focused. They may also model saving habits for others. Their frugality and saving secures necessities for the future.

Shadow Traits: Sometimes they care too much about money and don't want to share or try new things. Their frugality might be more about controlling others or showing off than being smart with money.

Themes: Themes could revolve around security and control.

Plot: The plot could be about someone who's holding tightly to their resources or status or fears change.

Story Conflict: The challenge might deal with fear of losing what they have or learning to share with others.

Relationship Conflict: They might have trouble getting along with others because they don't want to share or try new things.

FIVE OF PENTACLES

Basic Meaning: Represents tough times with money, feeling left out, or not having enough.

Character: Depicts a character who's a survivor or someone with a strong spirit.

Positive Traits: This character is tough and can handle hard times. They find creative ways to get by and care about others who are struggling. They believe in community support and helping each other out. When offering help, they take care to maintain the dignity of the vulnerable.

Shadow Traits: Sometimes they feel hopeless or depend too much on others. They might blame themselves or others for their problems and wallow instead of trying to find solutions.

Themes: Themes revolve around loss, isolation, and exile.

Plot: The story could be about someone going through a period of hardship or lack, or needing help from others, even if it comes with a risk.

Story Conflict: The challenge might deal with not having enough or a character having to ask for help when they need it.

Relationship Conflict: A character might feel alone or abandoned by others, especially when they need help the most, or they might feel like they don't belong in their community.

SIX OF PENTACLES

Basic Meaning: Represents generosity and helping others, either through charity, swapping skills or sharing resources. This card can also signify karma.

Character: Depicts a character who gives back to their community, like a philanthropist, patron of the arts, or someone who supports others.

Positive Traits: This person is supportive and fair and loves to help people. They feel that there's enough for everyone and want to uplift those in need. They believe that giving helps people become empowered, not dependent.

Shadow Traits: However, they can also be patronizing or controlling with aid. Conspicuous donations they've made serve their ego and status more than the cause they support. They might expect something in return for their generosity or believe that their charity absolves their responsibility for the root causes of the scarcity.

Themes: Themes involve charity, generosity, and motivations for generosity.

Plot: The story could involve sharing resources or knowledge with others or receiving help from someone else, perhaps in a setting where it's not safe to trust others.

Story Conflict: The challenge might be deciding who to help or how much to give, or dealing with someone who gives to manipulate others.

Relationship Conflict: Characters might struggle to balance giving and receiving in their relationships. This may show up in a relationship where there's an imbalance of power like an upstairs/downstairs relationship.

SEVEN OF PENTACLES

Basic Meaning: Represents pausing to reflect, assessing progress, and awaiting results of efforts. This card also signifies waiting to harvest and long-term thinking.

Character: Depicts a character who's wise and patient, a reflective practitioner, wise counsel, or steady caretaker.

Positive Traits: This character is patient and plans for the long term. They work hard and don't give up easily. They think about how their decisions affect everyone and use past experiences to do better in the future. They wait to see the full results of their hard work pay off.

Shadow Traits: Sometimes this character gets frustrated and feels like things aren't working out. Brooding and dwelling on past mistakes instead of moving forward is a common behavior. They might spend too much time analyzing every angle and not enough time doing. They may hesitate, endlessly reconsidering prudent next steps, afraid to take action.

Themes: Main themes for this card are patience, reflection, right actions, and investment in the future.

Plot: The story could involve someone checking how things are going or waiting to see if their hard work pays off.

Story Conflict: The challenge may involve a character's patience being tested or a delay in their efforts bearing fruit.

Relationship Conflict: Tension can arise because of delayed results or ongoing efforts. Characters can get locked into comparisonitis and overanalysis, or shrug off accountability. Each of these can cause conflict in relationships.

EIGHT OF PENTACLES

Basic Meaning: Represents mastery, apprenticeship, honing skills, diligence, perseverance, and perfectionism.

Character: Depicts a highly skilled person, a master craftsperson, passionate teacher or mentor, devoted learner, or accomplished artist.

Positive Traits: This character is hardworking and pays meticulous attention to details. They love what they do and keep learning because they enjoy growing. They want to use their skills to help others and contribute to their community. They like challenges that help them get better at what they do.

Shadow Traits: Sometimes they focus too much on minutiae, work too hard, or struggle with perfectionism, delaying their work because of unrealistic standards. At times, they care more about showing off than helping others. They might get upset if interrupted while working or if things don't go exactly as planned. They might work hard to impress others instead of feeling good about themselves.

Themes: Themes include diligence, education, and mastery.

Plot: The story could be about someone practicing to improve their skills or trying to meet a deadline.

Story Conflict: Conflicts may arise from the challenges of dedication and hard work or difficulty mastering a skill.

Relationship Conflict: They might have trouble balancing work and personal life, or they might get upset if someone interrupts them while working.

NINE OF PENTACLES

Basic Meaning: Represents feeling happy and comfortable, enjoying nice things, and being able to take care of yourself.

Character: Depicts a character who's really good at being on their own and doing their own thing, like a pioneer or someone who's independent.

Positive Traits: This character is self-sufficient and likes to enjoy the finer things in life. They work hard so they can have nice things and be independent. They're free to follow their inner callings, and still stay connected to others while valuing alone time.

Shadow Traits: Sometimes they spend too much time alone or focus too much on having nice things. They might care more about material possessions than people or avoid challenges that could help them grow. They might be afraid of getting close to others or depending on them.

Themes: Themes include enjoying or coming to terms with luxury and self-reliance.

Plot: The story could involve someone achieving success or finally being able to live comfortably after hardship.

Story Conflict: The challenge might be protecting what a character has achieved or dealing with the downsides of success.

Relationship Conflict: Characters may have trouble getting along with others because they're so independent or because they have more money than others.

TEN OF PENTACLES

Basic Meaning: Represents financial legacy, family wealth, traditions, long-term vision, and abundance in all forms.

The Character: Depicts a character who's a matriarch or patriarch, a visionary ancestor, or keeper of roots.

Positive Traits: This character is wealthy and has deep roots in the community. They care about their family and work together with others to make things better for everyone. They pass down their values and resources to future generations.

Shadow Traits: Sometimes they care too much about their status or are afraid of change. They might stick too strictly to traditions and exclude others. They might try to control what happens after they're gone and resist new ideas. Their rigidity can hold back the community from growing.

Themes: Themes include wealth and leaving a legacy.

Plot: The story could be about someone benefiting from family traditions or finding out something surprising about their family history.

Story Conflict: The challenge might be dealing with inheritance issues or conflicts within the family, like someone trying to take control of the family business.

Relationship Conflict: There could be tension within the family over inheritance after someone passes away, or there could be mysteries to solve about the family's past.

PAGE OF PENTACLES

Basic Meaning: Represents a practical student who's resourceful and eager to learn. Also, setting a stable foundation for growth.

Character: Depicts a character who's a resourceful student, curious apprentice, diligent intern, or methodical learner.

Positive Traits: This character is studious and practical, always eager to learn and find new ways of doing things. They work hard and make steady progress, enjoying the process of learning. They set a good example of how dedication pays off.

Shadow Traits: However, sometimes they're inexperienced and too cautious, sticking too closely to routines. They might care more about following rules than understanding why they're important. They might seek validation from others instead of finding joy in their work, and might complain instead of actively trying to solve problems.

Themes: Themes could revolve around ambition, apprenticeship, and learning.

Plot: The story could be about someone starting a new job or educational path, or a young character showing promise in practical matters.

Story Conflict: The challenge might be learning how to navigate the real world or facing obstacles early in their career or education.

Relationship Conflict: Naivety or inexperience might cause problems in relationships, or a character might be so focused on learning that they neglect other aspects of their life, including relationships.

KNIGHT OF PENTACLES

Basic Meaning: Represents being hard-working and reliable, making steady progress, and valuing craftsmanship.

Character: Depicts a character who is a skilled craftsman, always dependable and cautious in their approach.

Positive Traits: This character is thorough and consistent, always fulfilling their duties and persisting through obstacles. People trust them because they're realistic and practical, and they see their work as its own reward.

Shadow Traits: However, sometimes they're stubborn and slow to change, sticking too closely to routines and resisting new ideas. They might take too long to make decisions or focus too much on small details, which can slow down progress.

Themes: Themes include reliability, thoroughness, and relentless dedication.

Plot: The story could be about someone steadily working towards a goal, making progress, but maybe not as quickly as they'd like.

Story Conflict: The challenge might deal with a character's cautious nature or struggling to adapt to changes.

Relationship Conflict: Clashes might come from differing paces or approaches to life and work. Tensions could also flare over conflicts between duty and following one's dreams.

QUEEN OF PENTACLES

Basic Meaning: Represents abundance, nurturing, and valuing possessions. It can also signify someone who is down-to-earth and in touch with sensuality and the physical world.

Character: Depicts a character who's a generous host, inspiring matriarch, community sustainer, gardener, or cook of comfort food.

Positive Traits: This character is nurturing, sensual, grounded, resourceful, and makes the best of what they have. They inspire others to do their best and turn challenges into opportunities. They love taking care of others and find joy in nourishing them.

Shadow Traits: However, they can also be too controlling or focused on material things. They run the risk of becoming frazzled and overwhelmed, and then resentful from taking on too much to maintain the appearance that they've got it all together. They might resist change and be overly attached to their possessions.

Themes: Themes include practicality, nurturing, contending with overwhelm or the pressure to have it all together.

Plot: The story could be about someone providing support and stability, in their home or with their finances.

Story Conflict: The challenge might be balancing their need to care for others with their own needs or dealing with conflicts within their family or household.

Relationship Conflict: Characters might struggle to manage family matters or clash with others over how to allocate resources. They might also find that their nurturing nature leads to dependence and failure to launch behavior in their relationships.

KING OF PENTACLES

Basic Meaning: Represents being a successful leader, managing resources wisely, and achieving tangible goals.

Character: Depicts a character who's an altruistic, visionary leader, and someone who cares about the prosperity of their community.

Positive Traits: This character is successful, reliable, and accomplished, inspiring others with their vision and ensuring everyone has access to opportunities. They uphold high standards and strengthen the dignity of work for everyone.

Shadow Traits: Sometimes they can be too authoritative or focused on material things. They might use their authority to control others or prioritize assets over empathy and understanding.

Themes: Themes could revolve around success, discipline, and ensuring a legacy of prosperity.

Plot: The story could be about someone mastering a skill and achieving success through hard work and experience.

Story Conflict: The challenge might be dealing with responsibilities or the ethical dilemmas that come with power and wealth.

Relationship Conflict: Characters might struggle with power dynamics in their relationships or clash with others over investments and financial decisions.

CHAPTER 7.7
TAROT NUMEROLOGY

Here's a summary of the meanings of the numbers in tarot, focusing on the Minor Arcana:

ACES THROUGH TENS

ACES (ONES)

Aces are like the seeds of the suit. They're all about new beginnings, potential, and inspiration. They mark the start of something new, like a project or new phase, and carry a burst of energy, creativity, emotion, or ambition. If your character meets someone new in your story, drawing an Ace might mean it's a positive development, at least for now.

> Example: In one of my favorite paranormal cozy mysteries, *Eat, Pray, Hex* by Tara Lush, the heroine Amelia inherits a haunted inn in Florida. This story is full of new beginnings and Ace energy as Amelia discovers her psychometric powers, meets a new group of friends, and gets involved in solving a decades-old crime. This kind of new beginning is common in romance, cozies, and paranormal women's fiction.

TWOS

Twos are about finding balance, dealing with opposites, and working together. They show the need for harmony, cooperation, and making choices in life. Twos might represent a character struggling with conflicting desires or aspects of themselves they're trying to understand.

> Example: In the TV show, *The Chilling Adventures of Sabrina*, the main character Sabrina Spellman constantly has to balance her witch side with her human side. This mirrors the struggles often seen in paranormal stories, where characters have to navigate between two worlds.

> In books like the Sookie Stackhouse series and *Twilight*, vampires must contend with their natural instincts and bloodlust while forming relationships with humans.

THREES

Threes are all about growth, creativity, and working together. They show progress and the development of ideas, relationships, or projects. Or in the case of the Three of Swords, a blockage in this area: the loss of connection, grief over severed relationships, or stagnation of creativity. Threes might indicate that your character needs allies and friends, even if they don't realize it. They suggest a delicate balance, not as stable as twos or fours; however, that instability can lead to innovation.

Example: On the TV show *Charmed* and its reboot, the "power of three" is a big deal, showing the strength of magical collaboration between sisters. Threes might also signal a disruption of the status quo, like a new love interest or job opportunity that pushes a character into action.

FOURS

Fours are all about stability, structure, and building a strong foundation. They represent security, order, and feeling grounded in life. Think of the four seasons or the four elements (water, fire, earth, air). Fours might suggest that your character needs some time with a trusted friend to help them through a tough situation. They can also signal a moment of calm before things get hectic. Your character might also envy someone else's stability and wish for the same.

Example: In the animated series, *Avatar, the Last Airbender* the main character Aang must master all four elements to bring balance and defeat the Fire Nation, showing the importance of stability and balance in restoring peace.

FIVES

Fives signify change, challenge, and conflict. They represent upheaval, and the need to adapt to new situations. Fives are like mini versions of the Tower card from the Major Arcana. Not so fun in real life, but a great impetus to make our characters work for that happy ending.

Example: Way back in the first season of *The Walking Dead*, there's five energy when the main character, Rick Grimes, fights his way out of a hospital after a zombie apocalypse to find his wife and son. However, he discovers his wife has moved on with his best friend, leading to a lot of tension and conflict in the story.

In Taylor Jenkins Reid's novel, *One True Loves,* a woman finds love again and gets engaged after mourning her supposedly deceased husband. When she learns he's actually alive, she must figure out how to move forward.

In the TV show, *Manifest*, the lives of Flight 828's passengers and their loved ones are upended when the plane lands five years after it took off. While those onboard experienced no time passing, those left behind have lived five years, leading to messy and heartbreaking interpersonal situations.

SIXES

Sixes symbolize harmony, balance, and finding resolution. They indicate a period of healing, problem-solving, and the restoration of equilibrium.

Example: In romances with a hurt/comfort trope, a six moment might look like the two main characters coming to a place of harmony while one heals from an injury and the other cares for them.

In Lyssa Kay Adams' book *Isn't It Bromantic?*, childhood friends Vlad and Elena, who are on the verge of ending their green card marriage, find their way back to each other when Vlad gets injured. Elena returns to care for him, and being together in such vulnerable circumstances creates an opportunity for both physical and emotional healing.

SEVENS

Sevens are about introspection, reflection, and assessment. They represent the need to evaluate one's progress, learn from experiences, and make informed choices.

Example: Sevens are moments of breathing room within the narrative flow. Even in fast-paced thrillers or action adventures, too much non-stop action wears readers out. Sevens remind us to allow protagonists time to regroup and reassess their next steps.

In mysteries, and other types of crime novels, there are often beats with Seven energy after the sleuth finds out that their lead suspect could definitely not be the killer. Now they must take a step back and look at all the evidence again in light of this new development.

EIGHTS

Eights signify movement, action, and progress. They urge characters to take charge and move forward.

Eights carry a finishing energy that drives a character into the final push to achieve their goal. There's a momentum in Eights that serves as a catalyst to set The End in motion.

Examples: In the *Lord of the Rings* series, it's the main character Frodo and his bestie Samwise braving the last perilous leg of their journey into Mordor. It's the Losers Club in Stephen King's *It* banding together to face off with Pennywise for the last time.

NINES

Nines are all about nearing the end, reaching goals, and discovering oneself. They mark the so-close-you-can-taste-it, almost-there moment when success is within reach and potential is realized. However, they can also signify a near-miss. Nines remind us there are no guarantees in life and that stepping forward toward the risk anyway is an act of bravery.

Example: In romance stories, the grand gesture scene often has a strong Nine energy. At this point in the story, your character has grown and learned. They've reached a place of clarity and self-realization. Now's the moment they'll lay it all on the line and take a chance on love and an HEA with their person. It's

Julia Robert's character in *Notting Hill* telling Hugh Grant's character, "I'm just a girl, standing in front of a boy, asking him to love her."

TENS

Tens signal the end of a cycle, transition, and start of something new. They highlight the completion of a phase and the beginning of a new one, often with a sense of accomplishment and growth.

Tens of Cups, Wands, or Pentacles might mean the story has reached its happy ending, and they tee up epilogue moments where we get to see the characters in a place where they've come full circle after confronting their demons and growing.

With the Ten of Swords, you can probably tell by looking at the figure laid out with ten swords in their back, that this one lacks that sense of accomplishment and growth of the other suits. Events with Ten of Swords energy often show up at the All is Lost or Dark Night of the Soul story beats. They can also appear at a point within a series where dark forces prevail, setting up the conclusion to come.

Example: Think of the end of the movie *Avengers: Infinity War*. (Warning: spoilers ahead!) The villain Thanos may end with a sense of accomplishment, but things are looking dire for the Avengers heading into *Avengers: Endgame* with half of earth's population obliterated in the snap.

Also, the final book in Sarah J. Maas' Throne of Glass series begins with Aelin and her allies in some major Ten of Swords situations. Fighting their way out of the impossible makes the ending even more satisfying.

FUN FACT

Did you know that the meanings associated with each number in the Minor Arcana can also apply to the Major Arcana? For example, the Magician corresponds to number 1 and so on through 10.

For cards with numbers beyond 10, add the digits together. For instance, Death is card 13, so 1 + 3 = 4. This could suggest that the themes of structure and order are present in the concepts of death and rebirth.

THE COURT CARDS

The court cards (Page, Knight, Queen, and King) represent personality traits, roles, or situations.

PAGES

Pages embody the youthful, curious, and creative aspects of their suit. They point to new ideas, learning, and exploration.

> Example: Pages might show up as apprentices, Jedi padawans, rookies starting out in a new field, or grad students studying under an accomplished professor, like Phoebe and Rizwan in the TV show *The Irrational*.

> Many amateur sleuths in cozy mysteries have Page energy.

Pages are fun to pair with curmudgeonly or reluctant mentor figures to create tension and growth. Think of young scout Russell in the movie *Up* and how he annoys, challenges, and ultimately becomes a vital part of Carl's life. Likewise in *Spider-man: Into the Spider-verse*, Miles Morales embodies the Page spirit as he learns and explores his new powers. Peter B. Parker starts the movie as a jaded, out of practice superhero. Through Peter's relationship and reluctant mentorship of Miles, he's able to overcome some fears that broke up his marriage and derailed his life back in his universe.

KNIGHTS

Knights are all about action, movement, and energy. They're often associated with a youthful, adventurous energy. They represent the pursuit of goals, the willingness to take risks, and the drive to make things happen.

Knights make dynamic main characters and sidekicks because their intense focus on their goals sometimes leads to a "ready, fire, aim" approach that can create a lot of fun plot elements and tricky situations.

> Examples: Characters like the Norse god of chaos, Loki, Shawn Spencer from *Psych*, and Lucifer from the eponymous TV series have big Knight energy. Anthony Lockwood of the *Lockwood & Co.* book series by Jonathan Stroud and Netflix TV series also embodies Knight energy.

Pairing Knights with orderly and structured characters can create compelling friction due to their differing approaches.

QUEENS

Queens embody the emotional, nurturing, and intuitive aspects of their realm. They signify maturity, wisdom, proficiency in their field, and the capacity to offer support and guidance.

Examples: Here are some examples of characters from pop culture with Queen energy. Some play the role of queen and others do not.

- Georgia from *Ginny and Georgia*

- Evelyn from *Everywhere, Everything, All at Once*

- Shuri from *Black Panther*

- Lady Danbury and Queen Charlotte from *Bridgerton*

- Regina/The Evil Queen from *Once Upon a Time*

- Xiomara and Alba from *Jane the Virgin*

- Annalise Keating from *How to Get Away with Murder*

- Yenefer from *The Witcher*

- Michonne from *The Walking Dead*

- Circe from *Game of Thrones*

- Peggy Carter from *Agent Carter*

- Olivia Pope from *Scandal*

KINGS

Kings symbolize authority, mastery, and leadership. They represent the pinnacle of achievement within their domain and possess the ability to make decisive choices and inspire others.

Examples: Here are some examples of characters from pop culture with King energy:

- T'Challa from *Black Panther*

- Ben Stone and Jared Vasquez from *Manifest*

- Hopper from *Stranger Things*

- Roderick Usher from *The Fall of the House of Usher*

- Geralt in *The Witcher*

- Joel from *The Last of Us*

- Stan Edgar and Billy Butcher from *The Boys*

- Waymond from Everything, *Everywhere, All at Once*

- James Bond from the James Bond series

- Sherlock Holmes from the Sherlock Holmes series

- Jack Reacher from the Jack Reacher series

- Ben Song and Magic from *Quantum Leap*

Each card's specific meaning also depends on the suit it belongs to, but this can give you an extra dimension to consider when writing.

Chapter 7.8

Tarot Symbology: Common Tarot Symbols and Their Meanings

In this chapter, you'll find symbols that commonly appear on tarot cards along with their meanings. Looking deeper into the symbolic meanings of individual card elements can give you even more fodder to spark ideas for your story than looking at the cards as a whole.

SYMBOLS IN THIS GUIDE ARE DIVIDED INTO THE FOLLOWING GROUPS:

- NATURE SYMBOLS

- ANIMAL AND CREATURE SYMBOLS

- DIVINE OR SPIRITUAL SYMBOLS

- OBJECTS OR TOOLS

- STRUCTURES

Many of these symbols were popularized by the Rider-Waite-Smith tarot deck and its variants. Some entries provide examples of cards from this deck featuring those symbols. However, each deck has its own artistic interpretations and symbolic language. Additionally, certain entries include symbols not present in the Rider-Waite-Smith deck but found in other decks.

NATURE SYMBOLS

- **Flowers and foliage:** New growth, fertility, creativity, potential (the Empress, the Fool, Death, the Magician, the High Priestess, Temperance, Six of Cups, Ace of Pentacles, Queen of Pentacles)

- **Sunflowers**: Warmth, positivity, growth, openness, abundance, and adoration (the Sun, Queen of Wands)

- **Trees**: Growth, stability, longevity (Strength, the Lovers, the Hanged Man, Ten of Cups; in the suit of Wands, the cards often feature leaves growing from the wooden staffs)

- **White roses**: Beginnings, new starts, purity, truth, and spirituality (Death, The Magician, The Fool)

- **Red Roses**: Love, desire, passion, and vitality (The Magician, the Hierophant)

- **White Lilies**: Fresh starts, new phases, and opportunities for renewal. They can point to a need for honesty, integrity, or a higher moral grounding. (The Magician, Temperance, the Hierophant)

- **Vines or Ivy**: Growth, development, upward movement (the Empress, the Magician, the Hanged One, Queen of Pentacles, King of Pentacles)

- **Garden**: Fertility, abundance, creativity (the Empress, Seven of Pentacles, Nine of Pentacles, Queen of Pentacles)

- **Pumpkins**: Abundance, transformation, potential, illumination, protection, and growth (Three of Cups)

- **Pomegranates**: Fertility, abundance, mystery, wisdom, initiation, and spiritual rebirth. The balance of life and death, consciousness and the unconscious (The Empress traditionally has pomegranates on her dress.)

- **Sky (Clear)**: Higher wisdom, spirituality, intuition (the Star, Ten of Cups, Eight of Wands)

- **Sky (Cloudy or stormy)**: Inner turmoil, struggle, strife, conflict (the Wheel of Fortune, the Tower, Three of Swords, Five of Swords)

- **Water**: Emotions, intuition, subconscious (the Moon, the High Priestess, Temperance, the suit of Cups, Two of Swords, Ten of Swords)

- **Rain or Waterfall**: Cleansing, renewal, emotional release (The Tower, Ace of Cups, Three of Swords)

- **Rainbow**: Hope, spiritual connection, new beginnings (Ten of Cups)

- **Snow**: Isolation, difficult conditions, transiency, potential for rebirth after a dormant period (Five of Pentacles)

- **Mountain**: Challenges and obstacles, wisdom and enlightenment, progress, achievement and distant goals (the Fool, the Lovers, Two of Wands, Page of Wands, Eight of Cups, Ten of Cups, Knight of Cups)

- **Volcano**: Transformation, renewal, disruption, chaos, cleansing and creation, especially in the context of massive, disruptive change that ultimately gives rise to something positive and new (The Lovers in some decks)

- **Wheat**: Fertility, prosperity, labor and rebirth in a cyclical, abundant sense (The Empress)

ANIMAL AND CREATURE SYMBOLS

- **Animals**: Instincts, emotions, hidden nature (the Fool, Strength, the Star)

- **Birds**: Freedom, higher perspective, messengers (the Star, Ace of Cups, Nine of Pentacles)

- **Cats**: Independence, grace, mystery (Queen of Wands)

- **Dogs**: Loyalty, protection, instinct, intuition, carefreeness, playfulness, service, and devotion (the Fool, Ten of Pentacles)

- **Goats**: Fearlessness, independence, wisdom, transformation, virility and nourishment, Capricorn and Earth energy (Queen and King of Pentacles)

- **Snakes**: Transformation, rebirth, wisdom, temptation (the Lovers, the Wheel of Fortune, Seven of Cups)

- **Lions:** Strength, courage, power (Strength, Queen of Wands)

- **Wolves**: Tapping into primal instincts and intuition, asserting personal strength and power, solitude, independence, rebellion, and fierce protection, or fear of a predator real or imagined, which can trigger survival mode (the Moon)

- **Fish**: The subconscious mind, intuition, reflection (Page of Cups, King of Cups)

- **Lobster, Crayfish, or Crab:** Intuition emerging, primitive, unconscious urges rising from the depths (the Moon)

- **Horses**: A need to feel in control and drive a situation, freedom, power, vitality, guidance, and the start of a new journey or phase, willpower, drive (Death, Knights of all suits, the Chariot in some decks)

- **Rabbit/Hare**: Fertility, rebirth, intuition (Queen of Pentacles)

- **Spider:** Creation, patience, transformation, but also deception and entrapment

- **Stag**: Wild spirit, vitality, civility, masculine energy, independence (Though you won't find stags in traditional Rider-Waite-Smith decks, they appear in some modern decks on cards like the Emperor)

DIVINE OR SPIRITUAL SYMBOLS

- **Angel**: Guidance, protection, higher wisdom (the Lovers, Judgment, Temperance, Wheel of Fortune, Queen of Swords)

- **Clouds**: The divine, guidance, and protection (the Lovers, the World, Page of Swords, Queen of Swords, King of Swords, Ace of every suit)

- **Storm clouds/ fog:** Confusion, obfuscation, uncertainty (Three of Swords, the Wheel of Fortune, the Tower)

- **Cross**: Harmony, religion (Judgment)

- **Stars**: Inspiration, guidance, spiritual wisdom, a map, or plan (the Star, the Chariot)

- **Sun**: Consciousness, fulfillment, joy, enlightenment (the Fool, the Lovers, the Sun, the Hanged One)

- **Moon**: The unconscious mind, emotions, intuitive illumination, doubt, longing (the Moon, the High Priestess, Eight of Cups, Two of

Swords)

- **Crown**: Authority, attainment, and enlightenment (the Emperor, the Empress, Justice, Ace of Swords, Kings and Queens of all suits. On the Wheel of Fortune and the Chariot, the Egyptian headdress serves as a crown-like symbol)

- **Eye**: Wisdom, insight, awareness (sometimes featured on the Hierophant and the symbolic placement of the square in the third eye position on the crown of Justice)

- **Heart**: Love, compassion, emotional balance (Three of Swords)

- **Infinity symbol**: Eternity, endless spiritual rebirth (Strength, the Magician)

- **Tree of Knowledge**: Temptation, curiosity, lure of the forbidden and earthly pursuits (the Lovers often features the Tree of Knowledge and the Tree of Life)

- **Tree of Life**: The unknowable and ineffable, spirituality, the connection between heaven, earth, and the underworld (the Lovers often features the Tree of Knowledge and the Tree of Life)

- **Sphinx**: Mysteries, secrets, puzzles, riddles, integration, awakening, realization, and the overcoming of challenges (the Chariot, the Wheel of Fortune)

OBJECTS AND TOOLS

- **Cups/Chalices**: Emotions, creativity, intuition (the suit of Cups, Temperance)

- **Swords**: Intellect, communication, logic (Justice, the suit of Swords)

- **Wands**: Drive, energy, passion, action (the suit of Wands)

- **Pentacles/Coins**: The material world, wealth, prosperity, health (the suit of Pentacles, also called Coins in some decks)

- **Book or Scroll**: Knowledge, wisdom, awareness (the Magician, the High Priestess, the Wheel of Fortune). Some modern decks feature laptops which carry the same symbolism, such as the Hermit card in the Modern Witch Deck.

  - **Closed books or scrolls** may symbolize secrets. They can point to mysteries and concealed information that is not yet accessible.

  - **Open books and scrolls** represent knowledge opening up. When a scroll or book is open, as in the High Priestess card, it represents information coming to light, wisdom, and intuition for the seeker. The High Priestess offers access to concealed or hidden teachings.

- **Mirror/ Reflective Surface**: Self-reflection, insight, wisdom (the Hanged Man features a reflective sunlike disk behind the figure's head. Britt's 3rd Eye deck features a mirror on the Devil card, in which the figure on the card doesn't see her own reflection. This can represent addictions or ties to things that discourage or numb the capacity for self-reflection.)

- **Ladder/Stairs**: Advancement, progress, moving upwards (In the Light Seer's Tarot, the Hierophant card features a stairway to the divine. On the Death card in Lisa Kessler's Practical Tarot, a woman ascends stone steps, leaving a reaper in her wake..)

- **Key**: Knowledge, insight, answers (the Magician, the Hierophant, and the Hanged Man's body forms a key-like shape)

- **Staff**: Support, guidance, wisdom (the Hermit, suit of Wands)

- **Knife**: Severity, change, cutting through illusion

- **Candle or Lantern**: Enlightenment, wisdom, inner light (the Hermit)

- **Wreath**: Completion of a cycle, achievement, celebration, eternity, unity, honor, wholeness, and interconnection (the World, Four of Wands, Six of Wands, Three of Cups)

STRUCTURES

- **Castle/Fortress**: Security, stability, safety (the Chariot, Four of Wands, Five of Cups, Seven of Cups, Four of Pentacles)

- **House/Home**: Security, comfort, foundation (Four of Wands, Six of Cups, Ten of Cups)

- **Bridge**: Connection, transition, change (Five of Cups)

- **Tower**: Upheaval, sudden change, disruption (the Tower, the Moon, Four of Pentacles)

- **Gate/Doorway/Threshold**: New beginnings, potential, opportunities (Ace of Pentacles, Three of Pentacles, Ten of Pentacles)

- **Well or Deep Water**: Inner wisdom, hidden depths, subconscious (The Moon, The Star)

- **Ship/Boat**: Journey, life's voyage, moving forward (Three of Wands, Six of Swords)

- **Pyramids**: Structure, ascension, wisdom, protection, initiation, and mysteries (Knight of Wands)

- **Ladder or Steps**: Ability to connect to or move toward a higher plane (In the Light Seer's Tarot, the Hierophant card features a stairway to the divine. On the Death card in Lisa Kessler's Practical Tarot, a woman ascends stone steps.)

PART EIGHT

CONCLUSION

CHAPTER 8.1
CONCLUSION: MAKING TAROT YOUR OWN

Tarot has endured and remained relevant for centuries because it taps into something greater than any single culture or moment in time. The images and themes on the cards represent primal human experiences. The constant search for purpose and meaning that both unite and define us. Because of this, using tarot prompting allows us to go deeper into the psyches of our characters, creating fictional people whose flaws, struggles, and attempts to make sense of the world resonate more deeply with readers.

Meaningful connection has been a core theme in every story I've ever told, as well as an intensely vital facet of my life. I hope that the tools in this book have armed you with strategies to connect with both your readers and your creative side.

This practice was a hand that pulled me out of a dark time. We all need those, which is why this book exists. Thank you for coming along on this tarot and writing journey with me. If these principles, prompts, and reference guides aid even one of you, I'll be grateful beyond measure for the impulsive whim that led me to write this down (thanks, ADHD).

No matter what life throws at you, never lose sight of the fact that your stories matter. You never know when your unique perspective, your life experience, your hurts, and dreams and longings poured into your words will be a lifeline for someone else.

Whether it's through tarot or other forms of play, randomness, and novelty, may you always find your way back to the page. May you always find fuel for that spark that first called you to write and get your words into the world.

TAROT NEWSLETTER SIGN-UP

WANT MORE TAROT WRITING INSPIRATION IN YOUR INBOX?

Sign up for the Tarot for Fiction Writers newsletter and get a free bonus playbook, exclusively for subscribers.
Visit jessicaardencline.com or
jessicaarden.com/tarot to learn more

THE SECRET TO IRRESISTIBLE SCENES: A TAROT FOR FICTION WRITERS PLAYBOOK

Take Your Scenes from Mediocre to Must-read with these 19 Tarot Prompts

Want to create compelling scenes that keep readers turning pages and coming back for more? With the tarot prompts in this playbook, you'll uncover the secrets to crafting addictive, resonant scenes that hook readers and go deeper into your characters. This guide is designed to spark ideas with 18 high-impact scene prompts. Pair these with your imagination and tarot card interpretation to take your scenes from meh to must-read.

ACKNOWLEDGMENTS

Thank you so much to every single person who had a hand in bringing this book into the world.

First, a huge thanks goes to my Capitol Crimes (and Sisters in Crime) family. I feel so fortunate to be a part of this vibrant community of creative minds dedicated to helping one another. Thanks for your support and for giving me a place to road test and run with all my tarot ideas. Thank you also to Lisa Kessler for lighting my imagination on fire with the idea of using tarot cards as writing prompts. If you ever get a chance to take one of Lisa's classes, do it. She's a wonderful teacher.

I also owe a great deal of gratitude to my friends and writing community. My first readers, Sarah Bresniker, Terry Shepherd, Gina Mitchican, and Harriet Fox-Navarra offered vital insights that shaped this book into a more valuable resource. My weekly accountability group with Jennifer, Karen, Chris, and Sarah reminds me to look up and talk to people and keep moving forward. Getting together with in-person friends like Eileen, Judith, Lisa, and Catriona has also been a joy and boost to my well-being. Amanda Trejbrowski and Gina Mitchican, you two keep me sane and lift me up. I wouldn't want to do this writing or life thing without you two.

Next, I want to thank all 259 of my *Tarot for Fiction Writers* Kickstarter backers for your belief in and enthusiastic support for this project. You rock, and I truly appreciate every one of you.

Thank you to my editor, Emily-Lisa for offering encouraging commentary and catching the little things that slipped past my eyeballs no matter how many times I've re-read this manuscript.

I also want to send a shout-out to my "mentors from afar," who have been instrumental in shaping my thoughts about writing, publishing, and Kickstarter. My week always kicks off with Joanna Penn's Creative Penn Podcast. Joanna keeps on the leading edge of publishing and tech, and her interviews, solo shows, and Patreon content always make me think and inspire me. Anthea Sharp, thanks for your Kickstarter book, FB group, and helpful pre-launch feedback. Monica Leonelle and Russell Nohelty, your Kickstarter book, classes, calls, and Substacks gave me a blueprint for running a Kickstarter campaign and taught me so much about marketing and messaging. The skills and insights I've gained from you two gave me the tools I needed to level up and prepare for success.

Last, but certainly not least, thank you to my family, especially my husband Paul. Your dedication to our chaotic brood, unwavering support of all my crazy ideas, and steady presence are so vital to everything I do. Also, my two boys, Archer and Fisher, thanks for getting excited about this project with me. My parents always encouraged my love of books, writing, and making things (often messily) from before I could hold a pencil, and I'm forever grateful to you all too. Thanks to my siblings, siblings-in-law, nephews, and parents-in-law, plus all other family members and friends-who-are-family who've always been my champions.

ABOUT THE AUTHOR

JESSICA ARDEN CLINE

Jessica Arden Cline is a writer, educator, speaker, and tarot enthusiast, passionate about bringing storytelling and creativity to life.
Ever since picking up her first deck for a how-to speech on tarot while studying in Spain in the late 90s, Jessica has been fascinated by the cards' symbolism, wisdom, and interpretive power. She weaves tarot into nearly all her fiction, including her paranormal cozy mysteries and romance novels.

As an educator with over 15 years of experience teaching in university, corporate, and community settings, Jessica loves sharing her enthusiasm with students. She's also an active member, speaker, and volunteer at writing organizations, including Sisters in Crime.

When she's not writing, you can find Jessica dabbling in design projects, crafting, listening to Taylor Swift, reading, or sneaking off to the gym or coffee shop for some thinking time and stress relief. Mental health awareness has a special place in her heart, and she often shares her experiences with ADHD, anxiety, depression, and PTSD in hopes that others may feel less alone and seek out the help they need. As mom to her two neurodivergent boys and human to her German Shephard/ black lab puppy with 24/7 energy, there's never a dull moment. She also enjoys spending time with her husband, family, and friends, as well as researching creativity and exploring new places.

CONNECT WITH JESSICA AT JESSICAARDENCLINE.COM
CONNECT ON SOCIALS: HTTPS://LINKTR.EE/JESSICAARDENCLINE

ALSO BY
JESSICA ARDEN CLINE

THE TAROT FOR FICTION WRITERS SERIES

The Tarot for Fiction Writers series uses an approach that pairs your imagination with high-impact storytelling prompts and tarot interpretation. This method harnesses the power of play, randomness, and novelty, along with the archetypes built into the tarot to help you supercharge your writing practice.

ALSO BY
JESSICA ARDEN CLINE

TAROT FOR FICTION WRITERS:

USING THE CARDS TO SUPERCHARGE STORY IDEAS, DEEPEN CHARACTERS, & ILLUMINATE PLOTLINES

Reignite your creative spark and unlock your storytelling magic with Tarot for Fiction Writers.

Do unfinished stories feel trapped inside you, stalled by life's stressors?

Reclaim your inspiration and complete those books with Tarot for Fiction Writers. This illuminating guide taps into tarot's symbolic power to help you:

- **Unlock the Power of the Tarot**: Learn how tarot prompts can be used to break through writer's block and reconnect you to the joy of storytelling by leveraging play, randomness, novelty, and embracing archetypes.
- **Explore Tarot for Storytellers:** Get an overview of all 78 tarot cards tailored specifically to writers. Unlike basic tarot guides, this book contains interpretations revealing how each card can relate to characters, plots, themes, story conflicts, and relationship conflicts.
- **Master Tarot Techniques**: Follow step-by-step instructions on doing spreads to tap into your subconscious and your imagination, generate unexpected ideas, and deepen your narratives. The prompts and techniques can be used by both discovery writers and plotters.
- **Apply Over 200 Creative Tarot Prompts**: Use customizable spreads to craft compelling, multifaceted characters and relationships. Brainstorm deliciously complex plots that keep readers hooked. Inject fresh conflict and intrigue and overcome stumbling blocks.

ALSO BY
JESSICA ARDEN CLINE

TAROT SPREADS FOR FICTION WRITERS:

UNLEASH YOUR STORYTELLING MAGIC WITH TAROT SPREADS TO GET YOU UNSTUCK, MASTERMIND YOUR PLOTS, AND DEEPEN YOUR CHARACTERS

Unleash Your Storytelling Magic with Tarot Spreads

Are you ready to break through creative blocks and write the story you've always dreamed of? Get Tarot Spreads for Fiction Writers and revolutionize your writing practice.

This companion spread book brings to life the *Tarot for Fiction Writers* Prompt Library, featuring all 200+ prompts in full-page spread layouts designed to spark your imagination and guide your storytelling journey.

With collections of character and relationship prompts, plot, setting, & worldbuilding prompts, and prompts to get you unstuck, this book will help you:

- **Beat stagnation:** Get out of your well-tread paths with new perspectives.
- **Explore the hidden depths of your characters:** Craft complex, multi-dimensional characters with compelling backstories, motivations, and arcs.
- **Craft authentic and dynamic character relationships:** Explore the connections and tensions between characters
- **Mastermind your plots:** Develop intricate storylines, identify turning points, and uncover unexpected twists, turns, conflicts, and tangents that leave a lasting impression.
- **Add Tension and Subplots:** Throw obstacles in your character's paths.
- **Craft settings that do narrative heavy-lifting:** Hone in on settings that amplify conflict and enhance the emotional impact of your story.

ALSO BY
JESSICA ARDEN CLINE

TAROT SPREADS FOR FICTION WRITERS:

UNLEASH YOUR STORYTELLING MAGIC WITH TAROT SPREADS TO GET YOU UNSTUCK, MASTERMIND YOUR PLOTS, AND DEEPEN YOUR CHARACTERS

- **Brainstorm new story ideas:** Add an element of the unexpected to your ideation process.
- **Get out of the corner you've written yourself into:** Get unstuck and back on track faster.
- **Push through the "muddy middle" of a story:** Navigate lagging sections
- **Fill in holes during revisions:** Strengthen and tighten the narrative.
- **Overcome creative roadblocks:** Find fresh inspiration and reignite your passion for storytelling.

Whether you're a plotter or a discovery writer, these tarot spreads for storytellers are an indispensable tool for any fiction writer. Transform your ideas into compelling narratives. Let tarot spreads unlock the full potential of your imagination and bring your stories to life.

ALSO BY
JESSICA ARDEN CLINE

TAROT SPREAD NOTES JOURNAL
FOR FICTION WRITERS:

NEVER LOSE A TAROT-FUELED STORY IDEA

The perfect companion to the Tarot for Fiction Writers books. Record your spread notes in this journal.

PAPERBACK EDITION

6x9 inches, 120 pages, perfect bound

Contains 60 Tarot spread pages with space to fill in:

- Your story question or prompt
- Chosen cards
- Deck used
- Observations
- Meaning notes
- A blank page following each spread page to provide ample note-taking space

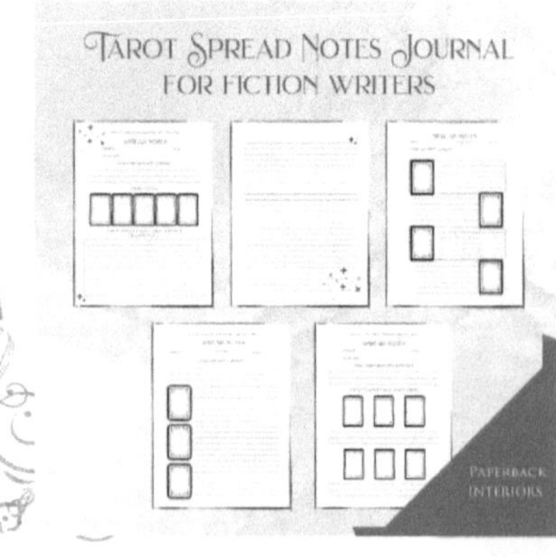

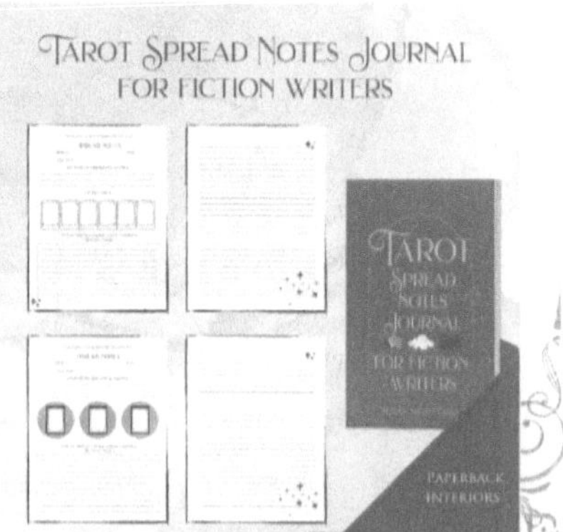

ALSO BY
JESSICA ARDEN CLINE

TAROT SPREAD NOTES JOURNAL
FOR FICTION WRITERS:

NEVER LOSE A TAROT-FUELED STORY IDEA

The perfect companion to the Tarot for Fiction Writers books. Record your spread notes in this journal.

DIGITAL EDITION

8.5 x 11 inches

The digital version contains six different spread notes layouts plus two designs of printable blank pages to use for additional notes. Each spread notes page features:

- Your story question or prompt
- Chosen cards
- Deck used
- Observations
- Meaning notes

Resources

Creativity, Stress, and the Brain

Books

Play: How it Shapes the Brain, Opens the Imagination, and Invigorates the Soul by Stuart Brown, MD and with Christopher Vaughan, MD

Iconoclast: A Neuroscientist Reveals How to Think Differently by Gregory Berns

Articles

"3 Reasons Play Is The Best Way To Develop Creative Writing" by Laura Stroud, Derbyshire Writing School, https://www.derbyshirewritingschool.com/3-reasons-play-is-the-best-way-to-develop-creative-writing/

"10 Ways Adults Can Be More Playful" by Kathleen Alfano, TheGeniusOfPlay.org https://www.thegeniusofplay.org/genius/expert-advice/articles/10-ways-adults-can-be-more-playful.aspx

"Benefits of Creativity and Play for Adults" by Albert Wong, Somatopia.com, September 30, 2023, https://www.somatopia.com/blog/benefits-of-creativity-and-play-for-adults

"Cognitive Flexibility: Neurobehavioral Correlates of Changing One's Mind" by Katharina Zühlsdorff, Jeffrey W Dalley, Trevor W Robbins, and Sharon

Morein-Zamir, Cerebral Cortex 33, no. 9 (May 1, 2023), https://doi.org/1 0.1093/cercor/bhac431

"Cognitive Flexibility Theory: Advanced Knowledge Acquisition in Ill-Structured Domains" by Rand J. Spiro, Paul J. Feltovitch, and Richard L. Coulson, InstructionalDesign.org, Accessed August 15, 2023, https://www.ins tructionaldesign.org/theories/cognitive-flexibility/

"Creative Writing: What It Is and Why It Matters" by Paul Jenkins, Brilliantio, January 13, 2023, Updated January 15, 2023, https://www.brilliantio.com /creative-writing-what-it-is-and-why-it-matters/

"Embracing Novelty is Related to Increased Creativity" by Joanna Poppink, LMFT, Belongly, Accessed February 11, 2024, https://belongly.com/blog/ embracing-novelty-is-related-to-increased-creativity

"Evoking Never Never Land: The Importance of Imaginative Play and Creativity" by Hayley Dominey, LEARNing Landscapes 14, no. 1 (Spring 2021), https://files.eric.ed.gov/fulltext/EJ1304947.pdf

"How Creative Writing Can Increase Students' Resilience" by Laura Bean, Greater Good Science Center at the University of California, Berkeley, October 30, 2018, https://greatergood.berkeley.edu/article/item/how_creati ve_writing_can_increase_students_resilience

"Novelty: Why It Matters and How To Embrace It" by joinreframeapp.com, December 13 2023, https://www.joinreframeapp.com/blog/novelty-why-i t-matters-and-how-to-embrace-it

"Play Basics" by National Institute for Play, https://www.nifplay.org/play-bas ics/

"The Creative Brain Under Stress: Considerations for Performance in Extreme Environments" by Oshin Vartanian, Sidney Ann Saint, Nicole Herz, and Peter Suedfeld, Frontiers in Psychology 11 (October 30, 2020), https://doi .org/10.3389/fpsyg.2020.585969

"The Benefits of Play as an Adult" by ProjectBoldLife.com, August 21, 2020, https://www.projectboldlife.com/the-benefits-of-play-as-an-adult/

"The Benefits of Play for Adults" by Lawrence Robinson, Melinda Smith, Jeanne Segal, and Jennifer Shubin, HelpGuide.org, Accessed March 1,

2024, https://www.helpguide.org/articles/mental-health/benefits-of-play
-for-adults.htm

"The Benefits of Play for Adults: 7 Ways to Play" by Justin Sunseri, JustinLM
FT.com, July 18, 2023, https://www.justinlmft.com/the-benefits-of-play-f
or-adults

"The Importance of Chance and Interactivity in Creativity" by David Kirsh,
Academia.edu, 2023

"The Importance of Play for Adults: Tips for Being More Playful" by Saya Des
Marais, PsychCentral, November 10, 2022, Medically reviewed by Danielle
Wade, LCSW, https://psychcentral.com/health/importance-of-play-for-ad
ults

"The Science of Novelty: How New Solutions to Old Problems Can Improve
Your Mental Health" by Alane K. Daugherty, Psychology Today, January 21,
2022, https://www.psychologytoday.com/us/blog/healing-stress-the-insid
e-out/202201/the-science-novelty

"Understanding the Psychology of Creativity and the Big Five" by Kendra
Cherry, VeryWellMind, May 25, 2022, https://www.verywellmind.com/th
e-psychology-of-creativity-and-the-big-five-5218513

"Unlocking the Cognitive Benefits of Play" by David Rock, Psychology Today,
August 11, 2022, https://www.psychologytoday.com/us/blog/your-brain
-work/202208/unlocking-the-cognitive-benefits-play

ADHD AND EXECUTIVE FUNCTION RESOURCES

BOOKS

*ADHD 2.0: New Science and Essential Strategies for Thriving with Distraction--
from Childhood through Adulthood* by Edward M. Hallowell and John J.
Ratey

*A Radical Guide for Women with ADHD: Embrace Neurodiversity, Live Boldly,
and Break Through Barriers* by Sari Solden MS, and Michelle Frank, PsyD

How to ADHD: An Insider's Guide to Working with Your Brain (Not Against It)
by Jessica McCabe

YouTube Channels

How to ADHD with Jessica McCabe https://www.youtube.com/@How-toADHD

ADHD is the New Black with Stacey Machelle https://www.youtube.com/@Adhdisthenewblack

Executive Function, ADHD, 2e. With Seth Perler https://www.youtube.com/@SethPerler

ARTICLES

"Executive Functioning Help" by Megan Neff, NeurodivergentInsights.com, Accessed April 11, 2024, https://www.neurodivergentinsights.com/executive-functioning-help

"Executive Function Issues: Possible Causes" by Gail Belsky, Understood.org, Reviewed by Laura Tagliareni, PhD, Accessed April 11, 2024, https://www.understood.org/en/articles/executive-function-issues-possible-causes

"What Does It Mean to Be Neurodivergent?" by Ariane Resnick, VeryWellMind, November 2, 2023, Medically reviewed by Ann-Louise T. Lockhart, PsyD, ABPP, https://www.verywellmind.com/what-does-it-mean-to-be-neurodivergent-5221391

PODCASTS, MAGAZINES, CONFERENCES, & THOUGHT LEADERS

The ADHD Artist Podcast with Sarah Gisen (Note: This podcast only ran for a year, but it is still well-worth listening to hear from other neurodivergent folks in the arts).

Women & ADHD with Katy Webber

ADDitude Podcast

ADDitude Magazine https://www.additudemag.com/

ADHD Paloozas: Online Conferences for ADHD Women and Couples https://adhdpalooza.com/

ADDdiva/ Linda Roggli ADDhttps://addiva.net/ (Note: In addition to her Get Organized decluttering program, Linda pulls together leading experts in the field to organize online conferences such as ADHD Women's Palooza and ADHD Couples Palooza. She's also a great advocate and resource for women over 40 with ADHD.)

The Shadow and Other Jungian Archetypes

Owning Your Own Shadow: Understanding the Dark Side of the Psyche by Robert A. Johnson

Writing the Shadow: Turn Your Inner Darkness Into Words by Joanna Penn

Romancing the Shadow: A Guide to Soul Work for a Vital, Authentic Life by Connie Zweig and Steven Wolf

Tarot History, Guides, and Resources

Books

Pamela Colman Smith: The Untold Story by Stuart R. Kaplan, Mary K. Greer, Elizabeth Foley O'Connor, and Melinda Boyd Parsons

Tarot for Beginners by P. Scott Hollander

The Magic of Tarot by Sasha Graham

ARTICLES

"A Machine for Telling Stories: Tarot and Speculative Fiction" by Carrie Sessarego, Clarkesworld Magazine - Science Fiction & Fantasy, April 11, 2024, https://clarkesworldmagazine.com/sessarego_04_20/

"Pamela Colman Smith" by Wikipedia, Wikimedia Foundation, Last modified October 26, 2023, https://en.wikipedia.org/wiki/Pamela_Colman_Smith

"Pamela Colman Smith: The Artist Behind the Tarot" by Patti Wigington, ThoughtCo, https://www.thoughtco.com/pamela-colman-smith-4687636 (accessed December 8, 2023)

"Rider–Waite Tarot." Wikipedia. Accessed April 11, 2024. https://en.wikipedia.org/wiki/Rider%E2%80%93Waite_Tarot.

TAROT RANDOMIZER WEBSITE

https://randomtarotcard.com/

Bibliography

Alfano, Kathleen. "10 Ways Adults Can Be More Playful." TheGeniusOfPlay .org. Accessed April 11, 2024. https://www.thegeniusofplay.org/genius/expert-advice/articles/10-ways-adults-can-be-more-playful.aspx.

Bean, Laura. "How Creative Writing Can Increase Students' Resilience." Greater Good Science Center at the University of California, Berkeley, October 30, 2018. https://greatergood.berkeley.edu/article/item/how_creative_writing_can_increase_students_resilience.

Belsky, Gail. "Executive Function Issues: Possible Causes." Understood.org. Reviewed by Laura Tagliareni, PhD. Accessed April 11, 2024. https://www.understood.org/en/articles/executive-function-issues-possible-causes.

"The Benefits of Play as an Adult." ProjectBoldLife.com, August 21, 2020. https://www.projectboldlife.com/the-benefits-of-play-as-an-adult/.

Berns, Gregory. Iconoclast: A Neuroscientist Reveals How to Think Differently. Harvard Business Review Press, 2010.

Brown, Stuart, MD, and Christopher Vaughan, MD. Play: How it Shapes the Brain, Opens the Imagination, and Invigorates the Soul. New York: Avery, 2009.

Cherry, Kendra. "Understanding the Psychology of Creativity and the Big Five." VeryWellMind, May 25, 2022. https://www.verywellmind.com/the-psychology-of-creativity-and-the-big-five-5218513.

Daugherty, Alane K. "The Science of Novelty: How New Solutions to Old Problems Can Improve Your Mental Health." Psychology Today, January 21, 2022. https://www.psychologytoday.com/us/blog/healing-stress-the-inside-out/202201/the-science-novelty.

Des Marais, Saya. "The Importance of Play for Adults: Tips for Being More Playful." PsychCentral, November 10, 2022. Medically reviewed by Danielle Wade, LCSW. https://psychcentral.com/health/importance-of-play-for-adults.

Dominey, Hayley. "Evoking Never Never Land: The Importance of Imaginative Play and Creativity." LEARNing Landscapes 14, no. 1 (Spring 2021). https://files.eric.ed.gov/fulltext/EJ1304947.pdf.

Graham, Sasha. The Magic of Tarot: Your Guide to Intuitive Readings, Rituals, and Spells. Woodbury, Minnesota: Llewellyn Publications, 2021.

Hallowell, Edward M., and John J. Ratey. ADHD 2.0: New Science and Essential Strategies for Thriving with Distraction--from Childhood through Adulthood. New York: Ballantine Books, 2021.

Hollander, P. Scott. Tarot for Beginners. B. Jain Publishers Limited, 2002.

Jenkins, Paul. "Creative Writing: What It Is and Why It Matters." Brilliantio, January 13, 2023. Updated January 15, 2023. https://www.brilliantio.com/creative-writing-what-it-is-and-why-it-matters/.

Johnson, Robert A. Owning Your Own Shadow: Understanding the Dark Side of the Psyche. Harper Collins, 1991.

Kirsh, David. "The Importance of Chance and Interactivity in Creativity." Academia.edu, 2023.

Neff, Megan. "Executive Functioning Help." NeurodivergentInsights.com. Accessed April 11, 2024. https://www.neurodivergentinsights.com/executive-functioning-help.

"Novelty: Why It Matters and How To Embrace It." joinreframeapp.com. December 13 2023. https://www.joinreframeapp.com/blog/novelty-why-it-matters-and-how-to-embrace-it.

Penn, Joanna. Writing the Shadow: Turn Your Inner Darkness Into Words. Curl Up Press, 2023.

"Play Basics." National Institute for Play. https://www.nifplay.org/play-basics/.

Poppink, Joanna, LMFT. "Embracing Novelty is Related to Increased Creativity." Belongly. Accessed February 11, 2024. https://belongly.com/blog/embracing-novelty-is-related-to-increased-creativity.

Resnick, Ariane. "What Does It Mean to Be Neurodivergent?" VeryWellMind, November 2, 2023. Medically reviewed by Ann-Louise T. Lockhart, PsyD, ABPP. https://www.verywellmind.com/what-does-it-mean-to-be-neurodivergent-5221391.

Robinson, Lawrence, Melinda Smith, Jeanne Segal, and Jennifer Shubin. "The Benefits of Play for Adults." HelpGuide.org. Accessed March 1, 2024. https://www.helpguide.org/articles/mental-health/benefits-of-play-for-adults.htm.

Rock, David. "Unlocking the Cognitive Benefits of Play." Psychology Today, August 11, 2022. https://www.psychologytoday.com/us/blog/your-brain-work/202208/unlocking-the-cognitive-benefits-play.

Rodari, Gianni. The Grammar of Fantasy: An Introduction to the Art of Inventing Stories. Translated by Jack David Zipes. 2nd ed. Teachers & Writers Collaborative, 1996.

Sessarego, Carrie. "A Machine for Telling Stories: Tarot and Speculative Fiction." Clarkesworld Magazine - Science Fiction & Fantasy, April 11, 2024. https://clarkesworldmagazine.com/sessarego_04_20/.

Solden, Sari, and Michelle Frank. *A Radical Guide for Women with ADHD: Embrace Neurodiversity, Live Boldly, and Break Through Barriers*. Oakland, CA: New Harbinger Publications, 2019.

Spiro, Rand J., Paul J. Feltovitch, and Richard L. Coulson. "Cognitive Flexibility Theory: Advanced Knowledge Acquisition in Ill-Structured Domains." InstructionalDesign.org. Accessed August 15, 2023. https://www.instructionaldesign.org/theories/cognitive-flexibility/.

Stroud, Laura. "3 Reasons Play Is The Best Way To Develop Creative Writing." Derbyshire Writing School. https://www.derbyshirewritingschool.com/3-reasons-play-is-the-best-way-to-develop-creative-writing/.

Sunseri, Justin. "The Benefits of Play for Adults: 7 Ways to Play." JustinLMF T.com, July 18, 2023. https://www.justinlmft.com/the-benefits-of-play-fo r-adults.

Vartanian, Oshin, Sidney Ann Saint, Nicole Herz, and Peter Suedfeld. "The Creative Brain Under Stress: Considerations for Performance in Extreme Environments." Frontiers in Psychology 11 (October 30, 2020). https://do i.org/10.3389/fpsyg.2020.585969.

Wigington, Patti. "Pamela Colman Smith: The Artist Behind the Tarot." ThoughtCo. https://www.thoughtco.com/pamela-colman-smith-468763 6 (accessed December 8, 2023).

Wikipedia. 2023. "Pamela Colman Smith." Wikimedia Foundation. Last modified October 26, 2023. https://en.wikipedia.org/wiki/Pamela_Colman_S mith.

Wong, Albert. "Benefits of Creativity and Play for Adults." Somatopia.com, September 30, 2023. https://www.somatopia.com/blog/benefits-of-creati vity-and-play-for-adults.

Zühlsdorff, Katharina, Jeffrey W Dalley, Trevor W Robbins, and Sharon Morein-Zamir. "Cognitive Flexibility: Neurobehavioral Correlates of Changing One's Mind." Cerebral Cortex 33, no. 9 (May 1, 2023): 5436–46. https:// doi.org/10.1093/cercor/bhac431.

Zweig, Connie, and Steven Wolf. Romancing the Shadow: A Guide to Soul Work for a Vital, Authentic Life. Wellspring/Ballantine, 1999.